BEYOND BROKEN

Finding Power in the Pain

Dr John Andrews

RIVER
PUBLISHING

River Publishing & Media Ltd
Bradbourne Stables
East Malling
Kent ME19 6DZ
United Kingdom

info@river-publishing.co.uk

ISBN978-1-908393-72-2
Cover design by www.spiffingcovers.com
Printed in the United Kingdom

Contents

Dedication

Simon,
My Brother.
Thank you for believing in me,
standing with me and fighting for me.
Forever grateful.

Acknowledgements

Beyond Broken has been the most challenging book I have written, as I have pulled back the curtains on the journey of my heart over the last few, painful years. I may have typed the words onto the page but none of it would have been possible without a world of support. The people around me continue to make me look much better than I am.

My first thanks go to Dawn, the love of my life. Your love and investment have made me a better man and your patience and support have made my writing possible. I love you with all my heart.

To Dan, Elaina, Simeon and Beth-Anne who make room for me to write and don't mind that I "disappear" when I do so.

Thanks to Helen Roberts for graciously agreeing to write the foreword. Helen and her husband Tim are among my dearest friends.

I am grateful to a band of unnamed friends whose love for me has never waned. Your relentless commitment to me has helped me overcome. You know who you are!

To Tim Pettingale for your patience, guidance and encouragement and to River Publishing for helping to bring my 13th "book baby" to birth.

My final thanks go to the Great Shepherd of my soul. In my darkest valley You did not leave me and Your presence, promise and power have carried me through. I offer You this book as a token of my thanks.

Foreword

Like an uninvited houseguest, or even worse a midnight burglar, brokenness can bash its way into our lives. Unannounced. Unwelcome. Unexpected.

Like the day I sat opposite a doctor and received his bad report. I tried to guess from his body language what he was going to say, but I couldn't. There were not enough clues to warn me of the news that was about to come my way. The "non-sinister" lump in my leg turned out to be masquerading and in one sentence I went from being alive and healthy to being told I was dying, sooner than I had planned. There had been secondary terminal cancer in my leg, a prognosis that propelled me to walk through a very dark valley. Doctors were unable to offer much help and, much like the woman who had bled for twelve years, I could simply reach out and try and grab the hem of Jesus' robe. Brokenness became that uninvited companion on a journey; a quest to discover Christ my Healer.

In *Beyond Broken* John Andrews takes us on a profound journey where we can discover a new wholeness from our brokenness and find *power,* even in the pain of our lives. Sharing his own phenomenal stories with transparency and humility, John walks us through lessons learned on roads that are hard to walk. This book is as refreshing as it is raw. It will help you. I wish I'd had it to read years ago!

For many years John has been both a friend and a hero to me. His love of the Lord, his passion for the Word and his ability to teach great and complex subjects in a simple way has inspired, equipped and helped me and many others to grow. Yet, it is in recent years that I've seen everything he has taught tested to the limit and, like the molten liquid in the refiner's fire, what has emerged in and through John is pure gold. John and his family have walked with honesty, integrity and fortitude and every page of *Beyond Broken* is a tribute to Christ's power within them.

This book will help you to make sense of what doesn't make sense. It will help you push through the opposition that threatens to overpower you and enable you to find victory despite the pain. This book will help you look up and beyond brokenness to discover wholeness in Christ, whose leadership is our ultimate example.

This brilliant book will shed light on your own path and guide you to a new freedom and victory as you step through the pain to discover Christ's purpose and power *Beyond Broken.*

Helen Roberts
Executive Minister, Wellspring Church,
*Author of **Be Victorious** and **Be Fruitful***

Preface

It was just after 6.00am and I sat in my living room in the stillness, my Bible on my knee and a coffee in my hands. A reading light dispelled the gloom and as the central heating kicked in, it slowly chased the early morning chill away. I felt weary, worn down by a decision others had made about me that I didn't understand and facing a family challenge that could only be described as a nightmare. In the silence, I sat back and looked up to heaven hoping for a word that might lift the burden. I lifted my Bible, kissed it, and spent the next thirty minutes or so reading the Scriptures before beginning to worship and pray.

As I was praying I was startled by a loud bang as something hit the patio window. When I investigated, I discovered that a small bird had flown into the window (something that happened a lot where we lived) and it lay on the path, stunned and apparently lifeless. I left the little bird and continued to pray, returning to the scene of the crash about five minutes later. As I looked at the "dead" creature, I noticed that it twitched occasionally, and by the time I returned a third time, the bird's head was up and it was starting to look around. Approximately ten minutes later I walked to the window, curious to see if it's recovery had continued and amazingly, as I did so, as if on queue, the little bird stood up, shook itself (I'm sure it looked straight at me) and flew away. As it did, the Lord whispered into my heart, *John, you will fly again.*

Every now and again we hit a "window", the result of which leaves us on the floor, stunned, disorientated and struggling to work out what just happened. The reason it happened isn't always clear to us, but even if it were, it wouldn't help heal the pain of the impact. These are defining moments that push hard against the person we are, the promises we've received and the purpose to which we are called. In the brokenness it's easy to get lost in the injustice of it all and become consumed by "righteous" anger towards those who have wounded us or let us down. Too many wonderful people have disappeared into the valley of disappointment.

This book doesn't ignore the reality of brokenness but rather embraces it, while making a journey of faith to help us find power in the pain. So often we pray for God to rescue us from the valley and "deliver us from evil". But what happens when the Lord doesn't *deliver* us and when instead of being extracted from the valley, He asks us to walk through it? Though this idea certainly isn't popular, it is biblical, as numerous heroes of the faith will testify.

As you walk with me over the next few chapters of this book, I pray you will discover that the Great Shepherd walks with you in and through the valley, whatever it may be.

"I was pushed back and about to fall, but the Lord helped me.
The Lord is my strength and my defence;
He has become my salvation."
(Psalm 118:13-14)

Dr John Andrews
August 2017

Chapter One
You Are Not Humpty Dumpty

"The Lord is close to the broken-hearted
and saves those who are crushed in spirit."
(Psalm 34:18)

When Elijah closed his eyes to sleep, his hope was that he would never wake up. Exhausted from an arduous journey and empty of all fight, the man of God sat under a tree in the wilderness with a single request: that God would take his life. All of this would have seemed inconceivable just a few days before, when this same man of God called down fire from heaven – the culmination of the boldness of his faith and the catalyst for a monumental victory.

But now, he sat alone. Now, his prayer echoed more with fear than faith. Now, instead of enjoying the sweet taste of victory, he dined on the bitter taste of defeat. Elijah, whose name means "my God is Yahweh" (*Eliyahu*), was broken. Even though he had heard the word of the Lord and fearlessly proclaimed it; even though he had seen the nation he loved so much, come to its knees before God; even though he had, by the power of God, emphatically defeated the prophets of Ba'al ... Now, by his own admission, he was finished.

As a child, like so many other children, I learned the nursery rhyme about Humpty Dumpty:

Humpty Dumpty sat on a wall,
Humpty Dumpty had a great fall
All the king's horses and all the king's men
Couldn't put Humpty together again

No details were ever given to me as a child about this rhyme, just the facts. I now know what Humpty Dumpty was, even though the image of an egg will be bouncing around in most of our minds right now. There is no clue in the rhyme as to his identity or the nature of his fall. Was he pushed, did he jump or did he just slip and fall? What we do know, as the tragic message of the rhyme tells us, is that no one could put Humpty Dumpty together again. Whatever the nature of his brokenness, it was beyond repair. Humpty Dumpty, it seems, was unfixable!

We have all had those moments when, metaphorically we've lain dazed at the foot of a wall, or sat disillusioned under a tree, and believed that the pain will never heal and the brokenness never be fixed.

The "fall" may have been our own doing, due to bad choices and behaviour. Or it might have been due to the actions of those around us. Alternatively, we might choose to conclude that it was just one of those things that happens in life. But whatever the cause, the consequences of brokenness confront us and, if not addressed, they will leave us in pieces, just like Humpty Dumpty.

Brokenness happens, even to good people. We can be doing the right thing, following after God, walking as righteously as is

14

possible, and serving our world to the best of our ability, when wham! Someone or something hits us, knocking the wind out of us and leaving us on the floor, grasping for an explanation and some empathy. As we lie there we're asking questions like, *What happened? Why did it happen? Why didn't God stop it happening? And why am I still on the floor?* ✔

The pain we experience can be so great that it challenges our revelation of God, the confession of the promises He has given us, and the purpose to which He has called us. In our minds we know the right answers, we know what we should do, but as brokenness takes hold, at that moment nothing makes sense.

Samuel Chand believes that, "...pain isn't the enemy. The inability or unwillingness to face pain is a far greater danger."[1] Within this statement lies one of our greatest challenges – that of "facing pain". Why doesn't God just take our pain away? Why doesn't He just rescue us from it and be done with it? Why should we have to face it? This is exactly where Elijah finds himself, with the choice of running from the pain or facing it. Clearly, he chose the former option, and why not? He would prefer to fall asleep and wake up in paradise, to his eternal reward, than to have to stay awake and face the issues that brought him to the foot of the broom tree. Elijah wanted to sleep away the pain. But the Lord had other ideas!

You are not Humpty Dumpty and you *can* be "put back together again". The journey beyond brokenness to healing and wholeness can sometimes be instant and miraculous. I believe in the supernatural power of the Spirit to touch and restore people instantaneously, and I have both seen this happen in others and experienced it personally myself. However, there are also times, when the journey to healing and wholeness means we will not be delivered *from* the pain, but *through* it.

Where recovery means the Lord doing a work in us that we neither expected nor wanted, but which was necessary all the same. In this process, we discover not only that there is life beyond brokenness, but that we can also find power in the pain. Whatever has caused it, "God never wastes our pain",[2] and He does not disregard our brokenness. Instead, He will use both, if we permit Him, to grow our faith, to enlarge our vision and to become more effective in His hand.

The part of Elijah's life that we are interested in is captured for us in 1 Kings 19:1-21. The passage tells us that Elijah,

"... ran for his life. When he came to Beersheba in Judah he left his servant there, while he himself went a day's journey into the desert." (v3-4)

We read these words so quickly, but the distances are staggering. The end of chapter 18 tells us that Elijah, by the power of the Spirit, ran all the way from Mount Carmel to Jezreel, a distance of 17 miles. But when Jezebel threatened him, he "ran" from Jezreel to Beersheba, a distance of somewhere between 100-120 miles, depending on how he travelled. Then, when he reached there, he went another "day's journey" into the desert, possibly another 10-20 miles. Before he stopped under the tree, Elijah had covered somewhere in the region of 140 miles. It's under the tree we hear his first fugitive words:

"I have had enough Lord. Take my life; I am no better than my ancestors." (v4)

But what would cause a man to run so far and say such things? As we put the whole story together, it seems a number of factors combined and conspired to produce Elijah's moment of brokenness.

First factor – His Expectation

If we look back into chapter 18 we can see the reason why Elijah may have entered chapter 19 of the story with high expectations. He experiences four dynamic events in chapter 18:

1. Fire. *"Then the fire of the Lord fell and burnt up the sacrifice..."* (18:38)

2. Victory. There are two expressions of victory here. He hears the people confess, *"When all the people saw this, they fell prostrate and cried, 'The Lord – He is God! The Lord – He is God!'"* (v39).[3] He also sees the prophets of ba'al conquered: *"... They seized them, and Elijah had them brought down to the Kishon Valley and slaughtered there"* (v40).

3. Breakthrough. The country had been without rain by the Prophet's word, but now it was time for rain to come. After prayer and the seventh time of asking, Elijah's servant reported the news: *"A cloud the size of a man's hand is rising from the sea"* (v41-45).

4. Power. One would think, after a hard day's work, that Elijah would grab a ride off someone to Jezreel, but as if to finish off a perfect prophet-like day we read, *"The power of the Lord came upon Elijah and, tucking his cloak into his belt, he ran ahead of Ahab all the way to Jezreel"* (v46).

On the back of fire, victory, breakthrough and power, Elijah walked confidently into chapter 19, undoubtedly fully expecting the Lord to take down Jezebel and seal the deal. But instead, she dug in and fought back, hitting the man of God with a punch he did not expect and sending him to the canvas of the desert.

Dislocated expectations can be devastating as they throw at us something we just weren't ready for. Elijah wasn't ready... and ran.

I can remember it like it was yesterday. I was serving in a dynamic, exciting ministry context and loving every minute of it. On my first working day, I stood behind my desk and knew I was the right person, in the right place at the right time, doing the right thing. Two years (almost to the day) later, I walked into a meeting to be told that, although I was loved and respected, my services were no longer required and the reason I was recruited was no longer an option. Growing up in Belfast I've survived a few fights and been on the wrong end of some beatings, but that morning it felt like I'd been hit on the head by a hammer and stabbed in the heart. The words bounced around in my head and everything seemed to go into slow motion. As a family we had burnt our bridges and jumped into this adventure with everything we had. Now all I could see was the exit sign!

As you can imagine, numerous conversations followed within my family, but one of the toughest was with my youngest daughter, who was thirteen years old at the time. To soften the pain I thought taking her out for ice cream might help. It didn't. In fact, as I placed the ice cream in front of her, without touching it, she started – she'd come ready.

I'll never forget her opening words: "If God told us to come here, why are we leaving?" I looked straight at her. I saw her pain and disappointment and at first didn't know what to say. Her expectations had been shattered. After what seemed like an eternity of awkwardness, I believe I received some inspiration from the Lord. I used the example of our Satnav (affectionately know as Sally). My daughter had travelled with me, so she had experienced moments when "Sally" had told us to go right, but for some reason that road was blocked. "What happens then?" I asked, "The Satnav reroutes," she answered. I tried to explain without crying that the Lord had told us clearly to "turn right", but for one reason or another that road was now blocked. However, God was rerouting us as we spoke. As I spoke the words, I hoped they helped her, but they were a balm of healing to my own soul. I heard my mouth say, "The Divine Satnav has never let us down and He won't start now!"

When our expectations are shattered, we are tempted to question the Lord, doubt ourselves and/or blame other people, but none of these things will fix the brokenness or empower us to go forward.

Elijah chose to run from the unexpected – a decision which almost cost him his life. Listen carefully to the words the angel of the Lord spoke to the man of God:

"Get up and eat, for the journey is too much for you." (19:7)

It seems the Lord had a new route already planned, but for Elijah to experience it, he had to listen to the Lord, look forward to where the Lord was leading him and leave his shattered expectations under the tree.

Our comfort in the midst of our unexpected moments is the knowledge that the Divine Satnav will never be caught unawares.

Second factor – His Emotion

In chapter 19, we get an insight into Elijah's emotional condition through four actions or reactions:

1. Fear. *"Elijah was afraid..."* (v3)

2. Isolation. *"... he left his servant there..."* (v3)

3. Exhaustion. *"He lay down under the tree and fell asleep."* (v5)

4. Paranoia. *"I have been very zealous for the Lord God*

Almighty... I am the only one left, and now they are trying to kill me." (v10)

What a deadly combination these four elements represent. We can see only too well how interconnected they are. Elijah's fear caused him to run, which led to isolation, which brought him to a place of exhaustion and, eventually, to draw conclusions that seemed true to him, but were actually wide of the mark. As Elijah's expectations crashed down around him, his emotions raged in every direction, causing him to make bad choices and come to some dangerous conclusions. Though a great man of God, carrying a powerful anointing as a prophet, the narrative now reveals to us that he was "a man just like us"[4] with fears, vulnerabilities and weaknesses. Elijah was in trouble!

The Word of God declares,

"The Lord is close to the broken-hearted, and He saves those who are crushed in spirit." (Psalm 34:18)

The Lord drew close to Elijah and stepped into his emotional melee and confusion, offering the means to calm his storm and restore his soul. He did so in two very different ways.

In the first, the Lord comes to Elijah

As he slept under the tree, the angel of the Lord came to him and touched him and said to him,

"Get up and eat." (v5)

He got up, looked around, saw some freshly baked bread and a jar of water, consumed them and then went back to sleep.

After a little while the angel of the Lord came a second time and touched him again and said,

"Get up and eat for the journey is too much for you." (v7)

This time he got up took the food and made a journey to

the mountain of God. Note some of the beautiful detail here through three elements of this encounter.

The angel *touched* him, *twice*. I don't think this inclusion is coincidental, but very deliberate. Remember, Elijah had left his servant behind and was completely alone. What the angel of the Lord did, his servant would have done. In the absence of human touch an angel touches the man, reminding him of his humanity and the fact that someone still cares for him.

The angel let him *sleep*. On the first encounter, the angel simply provided food and water then let Elijah sleep again. Remember, Elijah was exhausted. He'd been on the run for days, and from start to finish had covered the equivalent of five marathons. Good food and rest were needed to begin his restoration.

The angel *challenged* him. On the second encounter, we have the same routine, but this time the angel pointed the man of God to the journey ahead. Having allowed him to sleep, he did not want Elijah's sleep to become a coma. Now he had to get up and move from the broom tree of brokenness to the "mountain of God" and the prospect of hope.

When I left the meeting in which I was told my services were no longer required, I returned to my office, closed the door and sat down. Its stillness was in stark contrast to the storm raging within me. My eyes filled with tears and I wanted to cry, but I knew that if I did, I might not stop. It was approaching 11.00am and I still had a full day of work ahead with appointments to fulfil. My emotions went from confusion to sadness to anger to fear to confusion again. How was I going to explain this to my wife, my children, my mother and my world? Into my melee and confusion came the "touch" of a friend who walked every stage of the journey with me. Though I am so grateful for the support of so many in that season, outside of my family, Simon, became as the "angel of the Lord" to me on more than one occasion.

Though an extremely busy man himself, he made a covenant to stand with me, walk with me and help me work through the pain to a place of freedom. He never once asked me what I was going to do next. Rather, he was concerned with how I was now. I met with Simon often through those months, and hours were spent on the phone. His touch every time we met or talked was life-giving. Some days he just listened, other days he talked, but each and every time, he brought both comfort and challenge to me, relentlessly committed to making sure I didn't slip into a coma under the tree. He never let me get away with anything that wasn't wholesome and over and over again he said to me, "Finish well, finish well, finish well." Before this experience we had been good friends, but through this experience we became brothers.

In the second, Elijah goes to the Lord

The angel of the Lord pointed Elijah to the "mountain of God". Seems simple enough, until we consider what the journey entailed. The distance from Beersheba to Horeb is somewhere between 180-200 miles (as the crow flies), but if the journey was made via known roads, then that distance might double, which Elijah's forty day time-frame suggests. To meet with God he walked approximately 400 miles in 40 days. When he reached the mountain the Lord spoke to him in a still small voice and everything changed for him. The bread and water of the angel had got him to the mountain, but only the word of the Lord could empower him to go forward into the next stage of his journey. Elijah's willingness to move from the tree to the mountain, as difficult, painful and demanding as that forty day journey was, positioned him to hear the voice that would heal and re-commission him.

In the midst of my brokenness, my "still small voice" experience came through a book written by Gene Edwards called, *A Tale of Three Kings*.[5] In it he tells the story of the relationship between firstly David and King Saul, then King David and Absalom. They were stories I knew well, but now I read them with new eyes, tear-filled eyes. The still small voice of the Lord spoke loud and strong to me through its pages and two challenges came to me above everything else.

What do you do when someone throws spears at you?

Are you prepared to leave alone?

On the mountain, alone, before the Lord I had to answer these two questions, because I knew they would determine the rest of my life. And so, in His presence, provoked by His word, I answered.

I will not throw spears!

I will not cut the baby (meaning the church I was a part of)!

I expected that when the Lord spoke to me it would be to comfort me and make me feel better about myself, or perhaps to outline the super plan of blessing He now had for me as I went forward. But no... the word He spoke, in truth, I did not want to hear. Yet, I knew, even as I heard it, that it was life to me.

The temptation in our moments of brokenness is to run as fast as we can and as far away as we can from anyone and anything that might challenge our conclusions and our direction. But it was the *touch* of the angel and the *word* of the Lord that saved the man of God from slipping into a coma of oblivion.

In your pain, don't be afraid to let the angel of the Lord come to you, but don't be surprised if he arrives in an unfamiliar package. Don't close the door on those who truly love you, for their touch carries the gift of hope and their bread the fuel of life. In your brokenness, don't shut out the still small voice of the Lord. It may come directly from Him on a mountain, or it may come via His Word, a podcast, a book or a tweet. It's hard to listen when the pain is so loud, but His voice, however it comes, has the power to heal and restore you. I am grateful to Simon for being the "angel of the Lord" to me and for Gene Edwards for writing a book in 1992 that became God's "still small voice" to me in 2014. Both brought comfort and challenge and both helped me to move beyond my brokenness and from the broom tree to the mountain of the Lord and beyond.

Third Factor – His Evaluation

"I am no better than my ancestors." (v4)

   "I am the only one left." (v14)

In the midst of crashing emotions, it is not surprising that Elijah's view of himself came under pressure, as seen in the two confessions from his own lips. Both are striking in that they sit on opposite ends of the scale, reflecting perhaps Elijah's own confusion at that time.

Firstly, he under-valued himself – reflecting how he felt.

"I am no better than my ancestors." (v4)

This of course was simply not true, but in his emotional trough, Elijah fell into the trap so many of us succumb to, that of comparison. However, many of us also know that when we make comparisons from a position of emotional instability (high or low), the basis of our comparison is flawed and therefore the conclusion of any comparison suspect. Elijah's feelings are speaking in these words, and under the tree he feels like nothing but a worthless footnote in history that needs to be discarded like refuse.

When it comes to our own self-image, erratic emotions will always lead us to questionable conclusions. This is why we must not allow how we feel to drive what we do next. Many have quit ministry because they felt worthless, useless, under-valued or a failure. It is one thing to "feel" these things, but when they become our confession, they solidify into a cycle of negativity and lies that will eventually crush our spirits. I felt awful when I was dismissed from my ministry post. I felt like a failure having led my family into this adventure, only to have the wheels fall off. I felt afraid, wondering what the future would look like. I felt self-conscious, as I tried to second guess what people were thinking of me. These feelings all conspired to cause me to see myself as less than how the Lord sees me. I am a pretty secure person, but this experience pushed me to the very edge of my personal security – and at times I heard words come out of my mouth that sounded just like Elijah.

Secondly, he over-inflated himself – reflecting what he thought

"I am the only one left." (v14)

Again, this wasn't true, but Elijah believed it to be so. He was seeing the world through tear-filled eyes and a broken heart, so it is not surprising that what he saw wasn't quite how it was. Later, the Lord informed him,

"Yet I reserve seven thousand in Israel – all whose knees have not bowed to Baal and all whose mouths have not kissed him." (v18)

Elijah was not alone. He just thought he was. It is interesting that both elements of his evaluation come in the context of isolation. Alone, with no one to challenge or correct him, he under-valued and over-inflated. He was not worthless and he was not alone, but his was the only voice in the room, so it must be true!

Our brokenness will try to convince us that we are the only ones going through this and that no one else will or can understand. This evaluation only serves to strengthen our sense of isolation, which helped us arrive at this conclusion in the first place. As I looked at Twitter, Facebook and Instagram I was struck by the fact that planet earth continued to function as normal on my last day at work and everyone was having a great time, except me! That Christmas represented some of the darkest moments of my soul I've ever experienced. In those dark times I was sure nobody cared, nobody would ever employ me again and that nobody really understood. Of course, that was the darkness speaking, not the truth. The truth was I had an amazing wife and a wonderful family. I had friends who loved me and a whole world of people who believed in me, and I had health, strength and opportunities to explore. My challenge that Christmas season was reminding myself, "I am not alone."

Four months later, I was sitting in the sunshine enjoying a holiday in the Lakes with my whole family. It was our last holiday together before my eldest daughter got married. We had been out for our early morning walk/run and I was relaxing in the garden, reading my Bible. As I did so, the Lord spoke to me from a passage I had read many times, but now, in the routine of my reading plan, came fresh revelation that brought life. As I received the revelation by faith, it was as if the Lord filled my spirit to overflowing with joy and hope. I ran to

Dawn my wife and told her that my heart had been healed, that hope had been restored. However, every day from Christmas leading up to that day, I had to get up and confess that I was not worthless (even though I felt it) and that I was not alone. For four months I had to fight for simple truths that before had come to me so easily. I had to tell my mouth the right thing to say and remind my heart that I was not a failure. But now, in a moment of glorious grace, I knew I was no longer broken.

You are not Humpty Dumpty! He could not be put back together again, but you can. You are not unfixable and broken beyond repair. You have a hope and future in a loving God who does not want you to die under a tree, but experience His grace, mercy and power through His still and saving voice. I pray that you will know the *touch* of an angel and you will hear the *word* of the Lord.

"Failure isn't the end of the world for those who are open to God's tender, strong hand. It's the beginning of a new wave of insight, creativity, and effectiveness –but only if we pay attention and learn the lessons God has for us."[6]

Endnotes
1. Samuel R Chand., *Leadership Pain, The Classroom for Growth*, Thomas Nelson 2015, p.8
2. Chand., *Leadership Pain*, p.80
3. Their confession is an echo of Elijah's name
4. James 5:17
5. Gene Edwards, *A Tale of Three Kings*, Tyndale Publishing House, 1992.
6. Samuel Chand, *Leadership Pain*, p.194

Chapter Two
Walking Through

"My help comes from the Lord, the maker of heaven and earth."
(Psalm 121:2)

It was 11.35am on 3rd November 2016 and we sat nervously in a courtroom. The jury had deliberated for less than 45 minutes and we were called back in to hear their verdict. As we waited in silence for the judge to return, my son sat in the dock, his life in the hands of twelve human beings. The next words out of the mouth of the jury foreperson would have an impact on the rest of our lives.

The descent into this dark valley had begun on 29th May 2015 when we received a phone call whilst on holiday from Simeon, our son, to say that he had been arrested. An accusation had been made against him and he was calling us from home, having spent most of the previous night in a cell. Dawn took the call and I could see the horror on her face and hear the panic in her voice. We were miles away and our son was all alone, facing a life-changing charge. The five-hour drive home from our holiday was one of the longest of our lives. We drove most of the way in silence; we were numb, in shock, on the edge of panic as every imaginable scenario ran through our heads and we tried to comprehend what had happened and what we were going to do. Little did we know that the next eighteen months would push our marriage, our family and our faith to the very edge of their endurance. We were about to walk through something that, in my wildest dreams, I could never have imagined; a valley so dark that, at times, it felt like death itself.

David said,

"Even though I walk through the darkest valley, I will fear no evil, for You are with me, Your rod and Your staff they comfort me." (Psalm 23:4)

This psalm is often quoted at funerals because of its reference to death – "even though I walk through the valley of the shadow of death…". Ironically, the word "death" doesn't appear in the original text. A better translation is "in the valley of darkness", or "deep darkness", or, more poetically, "darkest valley".[1] The implication is that the valley is so dark that it *feels like* death – as if death itself were closing in on us – an idea echoed in the book of Job where this imagery is used as a euphemism for death.[2] But David wasn't talking about death in his psalm. Rather, he was referring to a life experience that feels like death with a valley so dark and so disturbing that a sheep could easily be lost to its darkness forever.

Valleys happen at some point in life for us all. We find ourselves in a place of darkness, even though we did everything possible to avoid going into it. The best of people have found themselves in valleys of sickness, grief, disappointment, rejection, accusation and discouragement. I would love to be able to offer you a theological "avoid the valley card", but there ain't one. Within the psalm, the experience of the darkest valley sits in the midst of promises of "green pastures", "quiet waters", "paths of righteousness", a "prepared table", an "anointed head", an "overflowing cup", and the reassurance that goodness and love will "hunt us down all the days of our lives". These are the bits we like and our eyes are inevitably drawn to the prospect of blessing and plenty, but we cannot contemplate the prosperity of the table without also accepting the "even though" of pain that the valley holds. In a psalm where the Lord is held up as *Yahweh Roi*, the Shepherd Lord, and where provision and prosperity abound, we cannot ignore the fact that at its heart resides the reality and challenge of pain.

As David walked through his darkness, he discovered some truths about *Yahweh Roi* that sustained him in the valley. There were things he discovered by revelation in the valley that he could not have found anywhere else. Even though he was not rescued from the valley experience, he celebrated the fact that he was rescued through it. In the eighteen months from May 2015 to November 2016, David and I walked together, and in the slow, painful journey through that valley, he reminded me again of four glorious truths about the Shepherd who knows the way, even in the darkness.

His Presence

"...for You are with me..."

As the dust started to settle around Simeon and the situation we faced, the conversations began and every one of them was terrifying. I remember the first conversation with our lawyer. As he laid out the process we asked him what the worst-case scenario might be, if Simeon was found guilty. When he answered, reluctantly, I didn't flinch (my pastoral training kicking in), but I wanted to run out and be physically sick. Fear gripped my heart as never before, as I considered the prospect that we might lose our son and that all the promise and potential of his life might be stolen. As I noted in the previous chapter, fear can make a person run away from what confronts them – but where could we run? There was nowhere to run, except into the presence of God.

In his psalm, David points to the fact that the only real solution to the fear that the darkest valley can create in us is the knowledge of the Shepherd's presence with us. David wasn't afraid because he was strong in his understanding of *Who* was with him. It was his faith-knowledge of that truth which chased the fear away. This is what we needed. It felt like fear was stalking us, waiting for any unguarded moment to pounce and devour us. Though we tried to live life as normally as we possibly could, we knew that if we gave fear an inch, it would take a mile and more.

My usual devotional routine is to rise between 5.30 and 6.00am on mid-week days and devote the first 90 minutes or so of my day to worship and the Word. I love the quietness of the early morning and the opportunity to set my heart again on the truths that will carry me throughout the day. It is a time I have enjoyed for many years, where on numerous occasions I have met with the Lord. As you might imagine, waking up to this new reality wasn't always easy, but I was determined not to neglect this precious routine that had served me so well in the past.

As I sat in that quiet place, I needed something from the Lord. I needed to see Him, feel Him or hear Him. My heart was heavy and my thoughts were going into overdrive. I knew that I had to be strong for those around me, but it felt as though at any minute, I might slip and fall. I kissed the Word and read it as I normally do, but felt nothing. Then I made my Word-based confessions, as I normally do, the platform for the worship that would follow, but felt nothing. I stood in His presence, removing my slippers as if on holy ground, and lifted my hands to heaven, but still felt nothing. As I worshipped I began to declare the greatness of the Lord over the valley we were in, speaking His promises over my family; that my "children would be mighty in the land".[3] As tears began to flow, as "deep called to deep", the word of the Lord came into my brokenness; a word I knew; a word I had heard before. But now it came as a fresh revelation of truth and power to assure me that He was with me. What was the word?

"I lift up my eyes to the hills – where does my help come from? My help comes from the Lord the Maker of heaven and earth. He will not let your foot slip – He who watches over you will not slumber; indeed He who watches over Israel will neither slumber nor sleep. The Lord watches over you – the Lord is your shade at your right hand; the sun will not harm you by day nor the moon by night. The Lord will keep you from all harm – He will watch over your life; the Lord will watch over your coming and your going both now and forever more." (Psalm 121:1-8)

I had heard that word two years before as I entered a lift, after leaving my brother in hospital. He had just been diagnosed with stage four pancreatic cancer and this had been my first chance to visit him since the news. As we talked that day about everything apart from "the thing", he suddenly asked me if I wanted to see his scar. As my brother lifted his shirt, what I saw so shocked me that I struggled not to react. That day we hugged, cried and prayed together and as I left him, the only thing I could see was the scar. As I entered the empty lift, fear jumped in beside me and for a few moments, filled the lift and my heart. I was overwhelmed. Then it happened. What I can only describe as a tsunami of love and grace flooded my heart, causing me to lift my hands and speak out this glorious psalm. As I did so, the fear left. Two years later the fear returned, but so did His grace.

Within this psalm we have five references to the Lord's covenantal name (*Yahweh*) and five references to the fact that He either watches or will watch over His people. The significance of the number 5 in Hebrew is that it points to grace and favour. Where fear abounded, the Lord responded with words of grace, and the assurance that He was with me and that He was watching over me. As we began our descent into the valley, this became the "Word of the Lord" to me. Whenever I felt the approach of fear, this was my confession. Whenever my heart felt like it would break, this was my confession. Whenever I felt nothing, this was my confession.

As David reminds us, in the darkest valley there is little light. We can't always see Him or feel Him, but those are the moments when we believe He is there, because He said He is with us. It's this truth that helps us experience the glory in the gloom as we hold on to His presence, irrespective of facts, feelings or fear. The Lord is with you. He has not and He will not abandon you. You are the work of His hands, the apple of His eye and the sheep of His pasture. Your name is etched onto the palm of His hand and your life is precious to Him. Fear wants to tell you that you are alone, abandoned and without hope, but there is a friend who sticks closer than any brother, and He is your Lord.

His Protection

"Your rod..."

My lowest point in the dark valley was the discovery that my son was self-harming. Due to the pressure of the process, he had descended into depression and was under the care of a counselor and taking medication. But in his darkness and brokenness, he numbed the pain of his heart by inflicting pain on his body. I confess this took me to breaking point. My wife, Dawn, was the true hero of this season, stepping forward with patience, love, strength, compassion and dignity at a time when the cuts on my son's arms were like wounds in my own heart. One "memorable" Sunday, Dawn rushed home from church to find Simeon sitting on the kitchen floor soaked in his own blood and when I saw the bandages around his arm I was overwhelmed with a sense of failure and guilt, broken-hearted by my own inability to help my son with his pain.

The shepherd's rod was there to defend and protect both him and his sheep from unwanted, nasty predators, so it might seem strange to talk of God's protection when some might suggest what we were going through with Simeon was evidence He wasn't doing a very good job. But my friend, Helen Roberts, who walked through the dark valley of cancer says this,

"By focusing on the hugeness of the opposition we can be left paralysed by fear and choose no action rather than steps of obedience; avoiding the challenge rather than pressing on and allowing the Lord to do what He wants to do."[4]

Facing the torment of a "thorn in his flesh", Paul pleaded with the Lord three times to take it away, but instead of deliverance *from* the valley, he received revelation *in* it:

"My grace is sufficient for you, for My power is made perfect in weakness." (2 Corinthians 12:9)

What a revelation it must have been to Paul, that the grace of God was sufficient for him. The word used here is *arkéō*, pointing to the idea of "enough", affirming that God's grace was all Paul needed for the thorn he was experiencing.[5]

What a revelation it must have been to Paul that God's power was made perfect *in* his weakness. The word translated "perfect" here is *teléō*, which carries the idea of bringing to completion and accomplishing something. The nuance of the word is not merely to end something, but to bring it to wholeness; to its intended goal. This is linked to Paul's "weakness" – *asthéneia* – a word which usually refers to weakness in relation to sickness, but in a more figurative sense can point to a feeling of impotence and weakness.[6] God's power came to completion in Paul through the impotence he felt because of the thorn. The thorn, it seems, was the means to a greater end! Of course, like all humans, Paul was focusing on the thorn, but it was through this revelation of truth that his eyes began to focus on the grace and power at work through the thorn.

God's grace was my rod. Though I felt I had reached breaking point, His grace and power was there to sustain me in my impotence. Trying to work it out and fight it in my own strength only led to greater frustration and pain, but in that moment I had to let go and confess, "I can't do this." The rod of His grace says, "So far but no further!" It protects us from that which is truly too much for us, and keeps us intact as we grapple with the thorn.

In an earlier letter to Corinth, Paul assured the believers that,

"And God is faithful; He will not let you be tempted beyond what you can bear. But when you are tempted, He will also provide a way out so that you can stand up under it." (1 Corinthians 10:13)

Paul's current experience was now proving this theology to be true, but it also demonstrated that the "way out" alluded to in this verse might embody itself through grace to endure rather than help to find the exit. I was discovering that His *way out* was in fact a *way through*. Though we did not ignore Simeon's cuts, we knew that if they became our focus we would never escape the valley. Somehow, we had to lift our eyes to see the Shepherd and the assurance that the presence of His rod meant, "So far but no further". As Helen concludes, "...victory comes when we take our eyes off our own inadequacy and look to God who is the source of our help."[7]

His Guidance

"Your staff..."

On the day we heard Simeon's case was going to Crown Court, we were devastated. Things had dragged on from May 2015. Although as a family we had tried to get on with our lives as normally as possible, we knew that for Simeon, life was on hold. Though the seriousness of the situation remained with us, the urgency had dissipated somewhat with the feeling that the case against him might be dropped. But instead, in March 2016 the bombshell was dropped on us.

In the dark valley we had learned to live with certain things, constantly hoping that at any moment the exit light would flash and we could make our way out. This news made the valley darker than ever. It was into this darkness that the light of Psalm 34 shone. Again, in the context of my normal devotions, the Lord clearly directed me to this psalm and it was quickened to me that I should make it the heart of my worship, confession and prayers for the duration of the valley. It begins:

"I will extol the Lord at all times, His praise will always be on

my lips. My soul will boast in the Lord; let the afflicted hear and rejoice." (Psalm 34:1-2)

It finishes with,

"The Lord redeems His servants; no one will be condemned who takes refuge in Him." (v22)

Every day until the final day in court, I read, recited, confessed, prayed and worshipped my way through this glorious psalm. During that time it became His staff to me. Just as the shepherd's staff was a sign of his ability to guide the sheep, so this word became a daily guide to my thinking and a challenge to my feelings.

Another psalm proclaims,

"Your word is a lamp to my feet and a light to my path." (Psalm 119:105)

Place that idea into the context of the darkest valley and we can see the power of His Word-staff to guide us when the light of the sun cannot penetrate to the floor of the valley; when the only light available to us is that granted by His Word and His Truth.

One word in particular in this psalm became my core confession. Verse 20 says,

"He protects all his bones, not one of them will be broken."

The Lord promised me that Simeon would not be lost to the darkness of this valley. That he would be saved because none of my "bones" (my children) would be broken or destroyed by this.

When all human light has gone, the Shepherd still knows the way. His staff is the symbol of His ability to guide us in the darkness and take us through the valley. In our pain and brokenness, His Word can form the light we need to take the next step and His Word becomes our guide on the path. Open His Word and let the light of His staff shine into your soul.

His Comfort

"... they comfort me."

Sunday 30th October 2016 was a challenging day. The trial started the next day, so I had booked a hotel for Dawn, Simeon and myself for the week, planning to arrive on Sunday night to be fresh and ready for court on Monday morning. We had asked our girls, Elaina (our oldest and married to Dan) and Beth-Anne (our youngest) to stay at home, as we didn't want to put them through the stress of the ordeal. I must say at this point that both our girls and Dan were amazing throughout. Their maturity, strength, courage and relentless commitment to the family are one of the factors that enabled us to get through. Two ministry friends, Professor William Kay and Pastor David Shearman, had asked if they could come and pray with the family before we left for the hotel. As they did so, those few moments were charged with compassion and tenderness, and with tears in their eyes, they covered our little family in prayer. I shall never forget their generosity and kindness to us!

The time came to say goodbye. We had to pack a bag for Simeon in case he was found guilty. As we hugged and cried together as a family that Sunday night, there was the unspoken horror lurking in us all that our son, their brother, might not come back. The drive to the hotel was mercifully uneventful as silence filled the car.

In the valley, the Shepherd promises to comfort us. The word used here points to comfort in a place of mourning and sorrow – the same word used in Genesis 24:67 when Rebekah comforted Isaac after the death of his mother, and in Isaiah 66:13 where the Lord promises to comfort Jerusalem as "a mother comforts her child." In both these examples the image is of tenderness being delivered via the intimacy of relationship.

The comfort comes through contact. Rebekah draws close to Isaac and the Lord draws close to Jerusalem. So this is at the heart of the Shepherd's comfort. In our mourning and sorrow, He draws close to us, alongside us, and through the contact of His tender touch, consoles us with His tender mercies.

What a thought to have in the darkest valley – that the Shepherd draws near to us, not because we are a commercial commodity, but because we are part of Him; we are His family. I love how the Lord puts it in Isaiah when He declares,

ᵎᐯ *"When you pass **through** the waters, **I will be with you**; and when you pass **through** the rivers they will not sweep over you. When you walk **through** the fire, you will not be burned; and the flames will not set you ablaze. For I am the Lord your God, the Holy One of Israel, **your Saviour**."* (Isaiah 43:2-3)[8] ᐟᐠ

Three times in this passage the Lord uses the word "through", but the hope at the heart of going through is the truth that "I will be with you."

He was with us in the courtroom as we passed through the waters and as the rivers tried to drown us. He was with us in the fire, when my son took the stand and the flames did not set him or us ablaze. When I woke on 3rd November the first book I grabbed was the Bible. As normal I kissed it, recited Psalm 119:18 and read the next chapters in my plan. That day, Isaiah 65 formed part of my reading, and from it, the Lord who was with us, our Saviour, graciously spoke to me one more time from verse 23:

"They will not toil in vain or bear children doomed to misfortune; for they will be a people blessed by the Lord, they and their descendants with them."

As the jury returned into the court breaking the tense silence, my thoughts were with my son who sat alone in the dock and my eyes looked to the Lord. A lady foreperson stood. She was asked if the jury had reached a unanimous verdict and she confirmed they had. The only words I can really remember after that were "Not guilty!"

Eighteen months of emotion erupted in tears of joy as we celebrated the fact that Simeon was free and we started to ascend out of the valley towards the light of the sun. That same morning, before we left for court, one of our dearest friends Rachel Field sent me a text. She said the Lord had spoken to her from Psalm 37:6:

"He will make your righteousness shine like the dawn, the justice of your cause like the noon day sun."

From this verse she believed that Simeon would be vindicated by noon, something that seemed completely impossible at the time, as the jury hadn't even been released to start their deliberations. Yet, remarkably, some might say miraculously, we stepped out of the Court building onto the street that same day at exactly 12 noon.

As I shared earlier in this chapter, from March 2016 to the trial I had been praying through Psalm 34 verse by verse. On what would have been the final day of the trial (it finished a day early), the day we drove home with our son, my Psalm 34 prayer/confession verse was this:

"A righteous man may have many troubles, but the Lord delivers him from them all; He protects all his bones, not one of them will be broken." (v20)

Whatever valley you are in, He is with you, whether you can see or feel Him or not. He will walk in it with you and He will bring you through. His rod won't allow you to be subject to more than you can bear, for His rod says, "So far but no further." His grace is enough and His power is brought to completion in your impotence. In the darkness, He knows the way, even if you feel you've lost yours. With His Word-staff, He will guide you, watch over and direct your steps on the valley floor. He will comfort you and console you in your mourning and "no one will be condemned who takes refuge in Him."

As you walk through, I pray, you will walk strong.

"We have escaped like a bird out of the fowler's snare;
the snare has been broken, and we have escaped. Our help is in
the name of the Lord, the Maker of heaven and earth."
(Psalm 124:7-8)

Endnotes
1. găy şăl·mā·wĕṯ בְּגֵיא צַלְמָוֶת
2. See Job 3:5, 10:21 & 38:17
3. Psalm 112:2
4. Helen Roberts, *Be Victorious*, River Publishing, 2016, p.96
5. John 14:8 – Philip asked to see the Father and believed this would be "enough" for him.
6. Romans 8:26 – The Spirit helps us in our *weakness*, our *impotence*
7. Helen Roberts, *Be Victorious*, p.96
8. My emphasis added

Chapter Three
#noneofthismakessense

"She gave this name to the Lord who spoke to her: 'You are the God who sees me,' for she said, 'I have now seen the One who sees me.'"
(Genesis 16:13)

As the blade of his father's knife touched his throat, Isaac must have hoped for a quick, deep cut from the hand of a skilful herdsman. Bound and helpless, he accepted his fate in silence and waited to die. The day had begun so positively as he and his father made their way to the place of sacrifice, but now through a cruel twist, Isaac realised he was the sacrifice! Suddenly the knife was gone and his father, in response to the voice of the Lord, now wrestled with a ram caught by its horns. The Lord had provided and Isaac was free. However, I can't help wondering what was going through Isaac's mind as he watched the ram's throat being cut. As its blood covered the altar, was there a sobering realisation within him that thought, "That could have been me!"[1]

Mount Moriah was a triumph of faith for Abraham. In Jewish theology this event is regarded as the last of the ten great tests of the first Jewish Patriarch, yet, with the exception of the writer to the Hebrews and James, there is hardly another direct reference to this story anywhere else in the Scriptures. And when it is mentioned, it is only in relation to Abraham's faith, not Isaac's.

"Abraham reasoned that God could raise the dead, and figuratively speaking, he did receive Isaac back from the dead." (Hebrews 11:19)

"Was not our ancestor Abraham considered righteous for what he did when he offered his son Isaac on the altar?" (James 2:21)[2]

As we read the detail of the account in Genesis 22, the Lord dialogues only with Abraham and it is Abraham who names the place:

"The Lord (Yahweh) will provide (Yireh)." (v14)

In the promise that follows this event, the Lord again speaks to Abraham, affirming the covenant of blessing with the assurance that through his offspring, "...all nations on earth will be blessed..." (v16-18), but nothing is said directly to Isaac.

If Mount Moriah was a triumph of faith for Abraham, I believe it was a trauma of faith for Isaac. In Jewish writings, this story is referred to as the *Akeda* – The Binding (sometimes *Akedat Yitzchak*), drawing attention to the fact that Isaac was bound up like an animal ready for sacrifice. From the moment of his binding, Isaac does not speak again in the story, and though the two men converse on the way up the mountain, not a recorded word is spoken between them on their way down back to the servants. In fact, there is not a single recorded conversation between Isaac and Abraham from this moment on until the end of Abraham's life. Later, Abraham provided a wife for "the son of promise" (Genesis 24) and left "everything he owned to Isaac" (Genesis 25:5) – all without apparent interaction.

It is striking that Isaac mourned for his mother, Sarah (Genesis 24:67) and needed comfort in his mourning from his new wife, Rebekah (Genesis 24:67), but when Abraham dies, there is no record of Isaac mourning his father; only that he buried him (Genesis 25:9-10). The suggestion that a gulf developed between these two great men may be purely coincidental, and over-reaching on my part, but there is little doubt that Isaac wasn't the same man after the *Akedah* that he was before. The silence around him is deafening.

Note the final statement in the *Akedah* before the narrative moves on:

"Then Abraham returned to his servants, and they set off for Beersheba. And Abraham stayed in Beersheba." (Genesis 22:19)

Where was Isaac? In fact, Isaac disappears from the text completely until Genesis 24:62 when it says,

"Now Isaac had come from Beer Lahai Roi, for he was living in the Negev."

Though no one can truly be certain of how old Isaac was during the *Akedah,* it is reasonable to accept that he was in his late adolescence or even a young adult. We do know he was thirty-seven when his mother died (Genesis 23:1) and he was forty when he married Rebekah (Genesis 25:20). It is striking that he's not referenced around the death or burial of Sarah, but that three years later when he marries Rebekah, he is still mourning for her. All this points to a gap, dare I say, a self-imposed exile, where the son of promise vanishes from the narrative, returning years later as a forty-year-old man.

The place of brokenness and pain can often feel like a like a liminal space, a gap in our journey where we struggle to find traction, direction or meaning, and where the much hoped for threshold seems to be alluding us. The word liminal comes from the Latin word *limen,* meaning threshold, and can be defined as a transitional stage in a process. To be in a liminal space is to be in the place in between, standing on the threshold of something new, while processing the challenge of now. As Rabbi Sacks put it, "It represents transition, and is marked by uncertainty and vulnerability."[3]

In our own liminal space, our family coined a phrase which often summed up how we felt: #noneofthismakessense. I have found this to be one of the greatest challenges of walking through the gap and processing towards a new threshold – that some stuff just can't be worked out and understood. Since 2013, I have preached at the funerals of my brother and father, walked through an eighteen month "trial" with my son, and negotiated two significant ministry changes. For most of these things I have no answers or explanations at all. In fact, the more I try to work them out, the more my head hurts! Friends suggested that whatever the Lord had for us in the future was going to be amazing, considering the journey we'd made. Although I was encouraged by this sentiment, it didn't help me with the now moment. Whatever new threshold there might be, and whenever it might happen, the reality of today must be addressed. It is our behaviour within the liminal space that will determine how ready we are for the next opportunity.

Pastor David Shearman once told me, "Our actions today are a prophecy of our tomorrow." This is certainly true of the liminal space, especially when it is laced with disappointment, pain and brokenness. Many have been lost in this space, unable to find their way or unwilling to go forward because, for them, their *Akedah* was too much to bear. I love how Rabbi Sacks positions this tension:

"We live our lives poised between the known past and an unknown future. Linking them is a present in which we make our choices."[4]

What choices, then, did Isaac make in his liminal space and how did he find his way beyond it to the threshold of a new day?

"Now Isaac had come from Beer Lahai Roi, for he was living in the Negev." (Genesis 24:62)

This might feel like an incidental fact until we realise we've come across this place before in the Genesis narrative. It's first reference is in Genesis 16:14 where the place was named as a result of a divine encounter that Hagar, the mother of Isaac's half-brother Ishmael, had experienced. She named God, *El Roi* – the God who sees me – because the Lord had "seen" her in her distress and rescued her. Hence the name of the place, Beer Lahai Roi – "Well of the living One who sees me".

Looking back on Hagar's experience from Genesis 22 we see some striking parallels between the two passages"

- Both Abraham and Hagar experienced an act of deliverance.
- Both Abraham and Hagar had a revelation of the nature of God.
- Both Abraham and Hagar put a name to the face of God by naming the place.[5]

What is striking is that both names given come from the same root word, but offer a slightly different view of God.[6]

Hagar's revelation was *El Roi*, "the God who sees *me*."

Abraham's revelation was *Yahweh Yireh*, "the Lord who sees what is needed and provides."

Hagar uses the more generic name for God, *El*, pointing to

the fact that perhaps she didn't know Him and this was the first time she had seen Him for herself. So for Hagar this is the first revelation of a God she did not know. Whereas Abraham uses the covenant name for God, *Yahweh*, because He knows the Lord and has already seen Him and established an agreement with Him. For Abraham this is a new revelation of the Lord he already knows.

When Isaac leaves Abraham he goes to Beer Lahai Roi. Maybe, like Hagar, it's because he doesn't really know God for himself and he needs to encounter the *God who sees me*. (No doubt he would have heard the story retold by Hagar as he grew up). For whatever reason, he can't see or celebrate *Yahweh Yireh*, and the narrative shows no spiritual activity between God and Isaac up to the point of the *Akedah*. Perhaps Isaac realised he didn't have the trust that his father had because he had not seen for himself the God his father followed? If Isaac, the one who brought laughter to his father and mother, was to make sense of it all, he had to find God for himself. So he goes to the place that represented Hagar's first encounter, to the place of the God who sees rather than the Lord who provides. To understand Isaac's journey through the liminal space of brokenness, we need to examine Hagar's experience.

Ten years had passed since the Lord had given Abram and Sarai the promise of offspring, but chapter 16 begins with an uncompromising reality:

"Now Sarai, Abram's wife had borne him no children." (Genesis 16:1)

Sarai, contending with her own liminal space, had, understandably, lost patience with the situation and offered a solution. Her servant would become her husband's "wife" and through this union, Sarai would build a family. It is striking that in the whole story, Sarai never speaks directly to Hagar nor uses her name. It seems the young Egyptian is just a tool in Sarai's hand. Abram agreed,[7] and the rest, as they say, is history. When Hagar found out she was pregnant, the narrative says:

"...*she began to despise her mistress.*" (v4).

The idea of the word here is to "consider lightly" or view as "less than". Sarai viewed this as a threat and secured Abram's endorsement to treat Hagar however she liked. We cannot be certain of the nature of the "ill-treatment", but it was bad enough for Hagar to run away, risking both punishment and disaster for her and the unborn child.

Hagar was on her way to Shur when the angel of the Lord found her. Shur was a town in the desert in the region of Northwest Sinai, positioned between southwest Caanan and the northeastern border of Egypt. Hagar, it seems, was heading home to Egypt, but the Lord had other ideas for her! This little spring in the desert of her brokenness and despair was about to become a well of revelation, hope and transformation.

From Ill-Treatment To Intimacy

Before this moment, there is no recorded conversation or connection between Hagar and the Lord. Undoubtedly "acquired" by Abram for Sarai when they were in Egypt (Genesis 12:16), her role had been one of bystander in someone else's story. Sarai oppressed her servant so severely that Hagar felt that escape was her only option, yet ironically it was in one of her darkest moments that she experienced intimacy with the angel of the Lord:

"*The angel of the Lord found Hagar...*" (Genesis 16:7)

Could this be why Isaac went to Beer Lahai Roi? Did he now identify with Hagar's suffering? Was his heart crying out to be found by *El Roi*, Hagar's God? The similarities between their experiences are striking. Neither of them seemed to have an awareness of God for themselves. Both of them were treated in an inexplicable way and both of them ran or moved away from their pain.

Psalm 116:10-11 records,

"I believed; therefore I said,
'I am greatly afflicted.'
And in my dismay I say,
'All men are liars.'"[8]

It is easy in our ill-treatment to both focus on those who are hurting us and come to the sort of sweeping and dangerous generalisation the psalmist admits to. When people let us down, betray us or ill-treat us, the natural temptation is to withdraw from all that reminds us of the pain. But we must be careful not to allow it to numb us to the intimacy of the presence of God. The "Sarai" and "Abram" in your life are not God, and their treatment of you is not the final say or the finishing act. There is One greater than them both, who can work in and through their behaviour, however inexplicable, to provide for you all that you need.

Though Hagar saw God, she only got the chance to do so because He found her and came close to her in her brokenness. Whatever it feels like and whatever has happened, El Roi is looking for you so that through intimacy with Him you can find life and hope.

Later in Psalm 116 it says,

"How can I repay the Lord for all His goodness to me? I will lift up the cup of salvation – and call on the name of the Lord. I will fulfil my vows to the Lord in the presence of all His people." (v12-14)

The psalmist had gone from focusing on affliction and that all men are liars, to calling on God's name and declaring His goodness. Only intimacy with the Lord can do this. Without intimacy we are left with ill-treatment and isolation, but through the power of His presence He can bring peace when, #noneofthismakessense.

From Run-Away To Return

As we've seen, Hagar was probably on her way home to Egypt, but when the angel of the Lord found her, He challenged her with a change of direction:

"Go back to your mistress and submit to her." (Genesis 16:9)

At first this sounds like the musings of a sadistic deity, but the next words out of the angel's mouth are the key to the request:

"I will so increase your descendants that they will be too numerous to count." (v10)

The Lord was not simply asking her to return to Sarai, He was urging her to hold on to her destiny, affirmed now by a promise of epic proportions. The Lord was not asking her to go back to the ill-treatment and humiliation (and there's no further record of ill-treatment when she returned), but to a place where the baby within her could grow and be nurtured, so that the purpose the Lord had for him and his descendants could be realised.

Isaac, the son of promise, was birthed miraculously from the loins of Abraham and the womb of Sarah, and one day he would have to return from his exile and take his place in the purpose for which he was designed. Just as Hagar returned a different person with the word of the Lord in the womb of her heart – a word that enabled her to submit to Sarai and give her son to Abram, willingly and freely – so when Isaac returned, it was vital that he carried more than the shadow of Abraham's revelation. For the sake of the future and the promise that lay within him, he needed to have the word of the Lord for himself.

When it comes to the work of the Lord, return is never about going back, but always about going forward. Whatever He asks us to return to, it is because He has something greater to reward us with. We may have run away from the pain, disappointment and frustration, but if the promise of God is within you, then at some point, the Lord is going to ask you to return. The return may not be to the *place* you ran from, but it will be to the *purpose* you left. Hagar returned immediately, whilst Isaac returned eventually. And to every broken pilgrim who believes that the answer to #noneofthismakessense is to run away, *El Roi* says to you, "You must return to the purpose I have for you."

From Abandonment To Acceptance

Abram's behaviour in this episode is, to say the least, pretty shameful. The great man of God shows his weakness and vulnerability on two occasions, both at the behest of Sarai. When she suggests a union with Hagar, the text tells us,

"Abram agreed to what Sarai said." (Genesis 16:3)

Then, when she blamed Abram for her suffering at the hands of Hagar, he responded,

"Your servant (Hagar) is in your hands... Do with her whatever you think best." (Genesis 16:6)

On both occasions, Abram goes with the flow, allowing pragmatism to drive principles, leaving their household, for a few inglorious moments, devoid of decency. Sarai may be the instigator in this sorry tale, but Abram shows weakness in leadership and disregard for his wife's servant. Though Hagar runs away, she does so because the man of God has abandoned her in his own house.

When the Lord sends Hagar back, there is a subtle but powerful change in the story. Note the language of the last two verses of the chapter:

"So Hagar bore Abram a son, and Abram gave the name Ishmael to the son she had borne. Abram was eighty-six years old when Hagar bore Ishmael." (Genesis 16:15-16)

In the two verses, Abram is named three times, Hagar twice and Ishmael (whose name means "God hears" or "listens"), also twice. Sarai is not mentioned. This cannot be a coincidence. For when Hagar returned, it was Abram who accepted her and her son, not Sarai. The meaning of Ishmael's name is further evidence of the cementing of this acceptance, as it demonstrated that Abram believed Hagar's story of *El Roi*, and the purpose now resident within his son.

There is also an interesting and potential controversial twist later in the story. After the death of Sarah, Abraham marries a lady called Keturah, and there is strong rabbinic tradition that Keturah was in fact Hagar, brought back to Abraham by Isaac, when he returned from Beer Lahai Roi (Genesis 24:62). She was given the name Keturah because "her deeds were as beautiful as incense" and she did not have sexual relations with any man other than Abraham.[9] If this is true (and as you can guess there are those who disagree), then this was the ultimate act of acceptance Abraham could bestow on the woman he so shamefully abandoned. The final sign perhaps of this acceptance is that Isaac and Ishmael stand side by side as they bury their father (Genesis 25:9).

I do not believe that Abraham abandoned Isaac as such, but

he seems to let the son of promise go too easily. He offers no post-Moriah explanation, no help or support, and if the silence of the text is to be followed, Abraham lets him go without much of a fight. Later, the great man attempted to make it up to the son of promise, by finding him a wife and by setting him up with wealth and opportunity, even sending his other sons away from Isaac, to give him every possibility to prosper.

Like Hagar and Isaac, there are moments when it feels we have been let down and abandoned by those we trusted and served. We find it hard to understand why they did not stand up for us, and why an agenda that didn't make sense was allowed to roll without someone, somewhere shouting "Stop!" But do not discount the work of the Lord to stir hearts, to change minds and to create opportunity for prosperity beyond anything we could manipulate or design. Remember, El Roi sees – not just the universe and the big picture, but He sees me, He sees you, and He sees the detail. He knows the truth, whatever the spin or the rumours, and He was there in the room recording every moment. He will see to it, that ultimately, the promise within you will find acceptance, and that which was once abandoned will find its place of purpose once again. When #noneofthismakessense and you're wondering what just happened, lean into the God of Hagar and the Lord of Isaac, who can make a way for acceptance where abandonment once reigned.

So as we leave Isaac, what might he say to us from his liminal experience, that can empower us when #noneofthismakessense?

Lesson #1: Even Promise Goes Through Process

Just because the Lord said it and started it, doesn't mean the promise won't be tried and tested. Isaac didn't just receive the promise, he *was the promise*, yet he had to journey through a trauma of faith and find *El Roi* for himself.

人 The promises over your life will be tested (if they haven't been already), but His word is sure and it will come to pass. Remember, 人

"God, who has called you into fellowship with His Son Jesus Christ our Lord, is faithful." (1 Corinthians 1:9)

Hold onto this truth in the moments when the process doesn't make sense:

"...He who began a good work in you will carry it on to completion until the day of Christ Jesus." (Philippians 1:6)

He is faithful to you and He will finish what He started!

Lesson #2: The Right Thing Can Sometimes Feel Bad

The triumph of faith for Abraham was a trauma of faith for Isaac. What "felt good" for Abraham was pretty awful for his son. Sometimes the right thing, the good thing, and even the great thing, doesn't feel so good when our experience doesn't match our expectations, and it wasn't quite what we hoped it would be.

Whatever it feels like and however it pans out, the right thing is always the right thing, no matter what. We have sometimes ended up with the nasty end of the stick, even though we did the right thing, but we must encourage our hearts and comfort ourselves with the truth that the right thing was still the right thing.

Lesson #3: We Can't Live Off Someone Else's Revelation

Abraham knew the Lord and saw Him as *Yahweh Yireh*, but there's no evidence that Isaac heard or saw the same thing. Isaac had to see the Lord, learn to hear His voice and be able to build his own altars and make his own oaths. In the days that followed, the Lord who spoke on Moriah would be known as the God of "Abraham, *Isaac* and Jacob", an affirmation indeed that somewhere in the liminal space, the Lord found Isaac and Isaac saw the Lord.

In our moments of brokenness, the pain will search the deepest recesses of our hearts to ask what we really know about the Lord. We cannot escape this question and we must answer it with humility and honesty. As the pressure is applied, what we truly see will come to the fore, and what we thought we saw, or hoped we saw, will dissipate under the pressure. If brokenness has done anything for me, it has affirmed what I truly see and made me hungry for what I don't!

Knowing is truly one of the greatest keys to going. It was what Abraham knew about the Lord that took him up Moriah to "kill" his own son and it was what he discovered about the Lord on the mountain that enabled him to go forward from that moment. It is interesting too, that God came to know something that day, for as Abraham reached out to kill his son, the angel of the Lord said:

"Now I know..." (Genesis 22:12)

Moriah, with its paradox of glory and gore, was not just about showing what was in the heart of Abraham, it was also about getting to the heart of Isaac. The Lord wanted to know what was in both men's hearts and the only way He could truly see was to place an altar that did not make sense to either of them, at the centre of their experience.

The writer to the Hebrews says of Isaac:

"By faith, Isaac blessed Jacob and Esau in regard to the future." (Hebrews 11:20)

In the post-Moriah liminal space, Isaac found peace and

ultimately found his place, playing his part and investing into the future. For Isaac, the trauma of the moment that did not make sense didn't destroy him, but it did define him.

Endnotes
1. Genesis 22:1-19
2. Hebrews 11:17-19 & James 2:20-24
3. Rabbi Jonathan Sacks, *Covenant and Conversation: Genesis*, Maggid Book, 2009, p.185.
4. Rabbi Jonathan Sacks, *Covenant and Conversation: Genesis*, pp.280-281
5. It is not clear whether Hagar named it or others on hearing of her experience, although she does name God.
6. רָאָה (rā·'ā(h))
7. See Genesis 3:17... same word used of Adam agreeing with Eve, the implication being that both men agreed to something they should not have.
8. The word translated afflicted here עָנָה ('ā·nā(h)), is the same used when describing Sarai's treatment of Hagar.
9. http://thetorah.com/our-step-mother-keturah/

Chapter Four
The Saga of the Suite

"There is a way that seems right to a man, but in the end it leads to death."
(Proverbs 14:12)

In the summer of 2015 we made a decision to buy a new suite for our living room. The old one had lasted around fifteen years and served us well, but its best days were behind it. Plus we had just moved house and so it felt like a good time to take the plunge and treat ourselves. We shopped around, as you do, and eventually found a stunning brown leather suite. We opted for a three-seater with two end recliners, a two-seater, both of which were recliners, and a single chair that rocked and reclined (that was really for Dawn. No one else is allowed to sit on it … at least when she's in the room). We went to a reputable firm (who shall remain nameless), spent a lot of money (which shall remain classified) and to be sure, we took out a special, five-year insurance policy, just in case something went wrong with our seemingly indestructible suite. It was eventually delivered in October 2015 and we all fell in love with it, even our Sausage dogs.

All was well until, after about eight months, we noticed that when extended, one of the recliners seemed to be slanting a bit and certainly wasn't as straight as the others. As the suite was under warranty, we contacted the firm we bought it off and they came and fixed it. All good. However, a few months later it started to happen again, but by this time, our warranty had just expired so we were directed to the company with whom we had the insurance policy. They listened to our problem, but told us they couldn't help us. I asked why and it was explained to me that because the same chair had been "repaired" under warranty, our insurance wouldn't cover it. Had it been another chair we would have been covered, but not *that* chair, even though we thought that chair was covered.

Just after that and just before Christmas 2016, one of the recliners on our two-seater chair stopped working (the one that I had claimed and loved sitting on … I should have claimed the rocker). I pulled the lever and nothing. So we called the insurance company and they assured us that someone would get to us as soon as possible. The repair man eventually arrived a few weeks later, took a look at our chair, took some pictures and informed us he didn't have the right tools for the job and left. The next thing we heard was that they wouldn't fix our recliner. When we asked why they said because the chair recliner expert who came out to look at it came to the conclusion that we had wilfully and deliberately broken it ourselves by some form of rough or inappropriate treatment. But this was my chair, the one I sat on, and that's all I'd ever done – just sat on it! I tried to assure the lady on the phone that I hadn't jumped or even danced on my favourite recliner, but she wasn't for turning. However, she referred my case to someone further up the chain, another very important expert on such things, who would make a final ruling.

In April 2017 we received a three-and-a-half page letter from the important expert further up the chain and in it she essentially said (and I summarise), "You broke it and we're not fixing it, so there. Oh, but you can appeal and here's what to do next." I was furious. We had spent a small fortune on the suite (still classified) and even bought extra insurance (that wasn't cheap either). And to add insult to injury, because it was *my chair*, I was the one, in effect, who was being accused of maliciously breaking it. Me, Dr John "I look after my stuff so well that it lasts forever" Andrews!

I know the saga of my suite reeks of "first world problems" (and I may not have too much sympathy from you when the planet is in such a terrible state), but incredibly, through this experience, I gained a fresh insight into my own journey of brokenness through the lens of my broken recliner.

I Did The Right Thing And Got The Wrong Result

This was one of the most frustrating aspects of the whole episode with my recliner – the fact that I had attempted to do everything right but didn't get the result I expected or deserved. We bought from a trustworthy firm, took extra insurance, followed all the protocols and in the end were shocked by the outcome. What I wanted to hear was, "Well, you're a good customer who spent a lot of money and paid on time and this is clearly just one of those things where something we didn't expect to break has broken, so we'll fix it." Does that sound unreasonable to you? All I wanted was to be able to enjoy Match of the Day with my feet up (unless Liverpool lose, then I go to bed early), but for some inexplicable reason, a chair that should not have broken, broke and all my good efforts and intentions, it seemed, were worth nothing.

Has that ever happened to you? You've done the right things but ended up with a nasty or unexpected result? Well you're in good company because it has happened to a few greats before.

- Abel offered God a sacrifice that pleased Him and got killed for it
- Abram left home for the land of promise and his first experience there was a famine
- David served and soothed Saul and had a spear thrown at him
- Jeremiah proclaimed the word of the Lord and ended up in a pit
- Jesus came to His "own" and, by and large, they didn't recognise or respond to Him
- Paul helped to plant the church at Corinth and poured out his life like a drink offering for them, so we feel his pain when he says, *"We are not withholding our affection from you, but you are withholding yours from us."* (2 Corinthians 6:12)

If we did something bad or wrong, we expect life or someone in it to give us a kick up the backside, and although that's never pleasant, it's not a surprise. But the challenge comes when we did everything we thought was right, good, fair and just and our reward is pain, accusation or rejection. Often, in such moments, we privately or openly invoke the Lord to our side with language like, "He knows", or "It's in His hands", or "He'll sort it all out". Of course, all of this is true and when spoken from a pure heart is a confession of life. But if we're honest, what we often mean by such sentiments is that the Lord will sort this out *for me*, because *I* did the right thing. *They* are wrong and sooner or later He'll bring *me* what *I* deserve." What we're expressing is a desire for justice or judgment, or if we're greedy, both. "If the Lord doesn't give me what *I want*, then may He give them what *they deserve*"!

But even if the insurance company that refused to fix my recliner had gone bust (not that I prayed for that), my problem would have remained, for my recliner was still broken. It is natural to focus on the injustice, but surely the priority is to address the brokenness that it has caused, and that is in our hands, not theirs.

I Got An Explanation But No Satisfaction

I received both a verbal and then a lengthy written explanation as to why the insurance company wasn't going to pay up and fix my furniture. They firmly believed their version of events, in which I had deliberately damaged a chair that I had just paid a small fortune for and they had photographs to prove it. But all the pictures showed was that my chair was broken, not how it happened or who did it. What they clearly weren't prepared to do was simply believe me, because as I was told, "A chair like this doesn't just break." I appealed to them on the basis of my character, my profession, my conduct, the condition of my home, and the fact I couldn't remember the last time I'd claimed anything on any insurance I had. My appeal fell on deaf ears, because they had made up their mind that I had broken it. After all, there's no smoke without fire. Though they had sent me an in-depth explanation (mostly generic), none of it gave me any satisfaction and my recliner was still broken.

What to do when you're not believed and when the facts

seem to point to one thing, but you know, because you were in the room each time, that how people think it happened isn't how it happened at all? This can cruelly add pressure to the weight of our brokenness – when a version of events is believed over and above the version you lived.

- Hannah prayed a prayer that changed the destiny of Israel, but the evidence convinced a man of God she was drunk
- David was fighting for Saul but the evidence convinced Saul he was plotting against him
- The Holy Spirit made Mary pregnant, but the evidence convinced Joseph that another man had
- Jesus was God in flesh, but the evidence convinced most of His world that He was just a carpenter, Mary's son

Over the years I've heard people express the idea that if only they knew why a certain thing had happened – why he/she did it, why they were fired etc. – that this information would help them to bring closure on their brokenness and pain. But I'm not sure I agree with that idea. Knowing why might help us to learn and, where possible, address issues and change behaviour and that's good. But knowing why won't help fix what is broken. In fact, in some cases it makes the brokenness worse. We can talk all day about why it happened, but the terrible fact is, it happened and something has been broken as a result. Finding out why will certainly inform you, but it won't transform you.

I was told why my recliner had broken and why they weren't fixing it, but it didn't help, because fundamentally I disagreed with their conclusion. I knew I didn't break it, but tragically, my recliner was still broken!

I Received An Apology But It Was Still Broken

When I received the letter from the expert further up the chain, I decided to give it one last go and I phoned the company. I was put through to a lovely lady who listened to me and responded accordingly. She was a highly trained professional and our chat, though strong, was friendly and amenable. At one point she said, "I am so sorry about all this," to which I asked, "So will you fix it?" to which she answered, "No, I can't." Throughout our conversation she apologised on three occasions in total, but each time refused to fix the problem. It was nice to hear "sorry", but frustrating that it was just a word.

For me saying sorry expresses at least one of two ideas, but ideally both together. Firstly, when I say sorry, I am acknowledging my words or actions, apologising for them and giving an assurance it won't happen again. Secondly, in saying sorry I take responsibility for what I've said or done and, where possible, seek to put it right. So if I break your favourite cup, I apologise for doing so, give an assurance I will never do that again and offer to pay for it to be fixed or replaced.

We see this in the wonderful Lukan story of Zacchaeus, an infamous tax-collector of his region. On encountering the transforming grace of Jesus, Zacchaeus announced,

"Look, Lord! Here and now I give half of my possessions to the poor, and if I have cheated anybody out of anything, I will pay back four times the amount." (Luke 19:8)

Now that's a sorry!

Even if we receive no apology, or the perfect apology, the challenge still remains that something is broken and needs to be fixed. A perfect apology will go a long way to helping that process, but even that is no guarantee that healing and wholeness will follow. The truth is, we can heal without an apology and we can remain broken with one, because deep down we know, our healing is not determined by the response of an apology from those who hurt us, but by the reaction of our own hearts.

Perhaps you've never had an apology and that fact has become, can I say it with all sensitivity, an excuse not to move forward. It has become your comfort blanket in your pain and your defence in the challenge. But hear me well, you don't need an apology to heal, rather you need to make a decision that what they did to you, justified or not, will not define you. Perhaps you did get an apology with bells on, but there is still a dis-ease in your heart. That's the realisation that what another person says and does has very little bearing on your ability to forgive and be free. Their apology may have been textbook, but if you are not prepared to let it go and cancel their debt to you, then you will be forever chained to a moment long past, that now lives on in your pain.

I Was Given The Option To Fight Or Fix

In the letter that contained the final decision of the company, I was offered the opportunity to fight the decision by taking it further, and to be fair to them, they included all the details of how to do that. However, looking at the process I knew it would take months of emails, calls, maybe another visit to the house and, of course, having to live with the fact my recliner was still broken. My pride wanted to fight and the Celt within me badly wanted to win, but I had a serious decision to make: to either fight a case that I may or may not win, or accept the fact that they weren't going to change their minds, and focus on fixing my recliner. We (Dawn still rocking comfortably in her chair), decided to opt for the latter. For us it was better to fix the chair than spend months fighting over it, while it remained broken, and we would rather be well, than win. People might say, "That's exactly what they wanted, for you to give in", and they could be right, but for us, the course of fixing was greater than the cost of fighting. There were more important issues in our lives at that time, so why allow something to steal our energy just because they had accused us of something we knew wasn't true? We decided to let them believe what they wanted to believe, but we would get on and fix the chair.

- What's more important to you, your reputation or your well-being?
- What's more important to you, saving face or living free?

There are times to fight, of course there are, and I'm not telling anyone not to fight, but before we go down that route, we must challenge ourselves as objectively as we can, understanding what the cost of such a journey will be. Over the years I have seen people fight so hard for their reputation and position, that in the end they've forgotten what they set out to achieve and become someone else in the process. Winning doesn't always mean finishing first, sometimes it means simply surviving and getting across the line. Our pride will drive us to cul-de-sacs of pain in which there is no guarantee that we will emerge with what we went in to fight for. What is worse, we might leave the cul-de-sac a lesser person than when we went in, diminished by battles that were more about winning arguments than building people. Be careful. Refusing to fight does not make you a coward. In fact, at that very moment, it might be the most courageous thing you've ever done. Refusing to fight could save you from the person you might become if you win, for there are some battles better left un-fought. If winning is your priority, then fight, but if the well-being of your heart is your priority, then think and think again. Some hills are not worth dying on!

It Got Fixed Even Though We Didn't Fight

A friend visited our home and he was reclining on one of the chairs that worked and, yes, you've guessed, Dawn was chilling smugly in her rocker! He's a skilled craftsman in another area so we asked his advice. Immediately he said, "I could probably fix it for you." He took a look at my poor little recliner and confirmed that he had both the tools and the expertise to put it right … sorted! In the end, that's all we wanted, for someone to help us fix our chairs. We didn't expect the process to be so difficult and stressful, and in truth, had we decided to fight, it may have been even more exhausting. But there, sitting in our world, was a good friend who had the means to help us and fix what was broken.

How often has that happened to us – that we've become so distracted by what's going on around us, the injustice, the arguments, the pain, the need to win and the fracture, that we miss the people in our world who have the ability to help us heal, regardless of the outcome? It might cost a little bit extra, and we might be annoyed we paid out in the first place, but all of that is forgotten once it is fixed. Be careful you don't become so consumed that you miss the obvious and ignore the opportunity. The Lord will see to it that there will always be something or someone in our world that can help us; someone whose primary concern for us is our well-being. I am deeply grateful that, on more than one occasion, such people have been there to help fix me.

Of course, we can be surrounded by amazing friends who want to help us, but unless we are prepared to take the right steps, even their generosity, commitment and expertise can't fix us. There are moments when winning means forgiving as we send away the offence meant for us and cancel the debt of those who owe us. When Jesus gave His life on the cross, He made only seven recorded statements, the first of which is captured in Luke's Gospel:

"Father, forgive them, for they do not know what they are doing." (Luke 23:34)

In forgiving them, Jesus chose well-being over winning in the way that the brutality of His world expected. Though nailed to a cross, He was the only free man in that place at that time. The subject of His forgiveness is *them*, and from this we get the clear understanding He's referring to all those present and represented. Yet no individuals are named and shamed. But what is important in our context is to see how He forgave them.[1]

He Forgave Them Without Being Asked

 If Jesus had waited for those around the cross to ask for forgiveness, He would have been waiting until hell froze over. After all, Pilate did the right thing in saving his own political skin. The Religious did the right thing in saving their religion from this rebel from up north. For the soldiers, Jesus was just another criminal who needed to die. Judas was remorseful because he had betrayed innocent blood, but he never apologised to Jesus. John (probably the youngest of the twelve) stood at the cross, but said nothing and Peter. Well, wherever he was, the friend of Jesus was most likely an emotional wreck, having used blasphemous language to deny he even knew the Galilean.

🗸 *No one asked and no one apologized, but He forgave anyway.*

He Forgave Them Without Any Acknowledgement

So what was the reaction of the crowd and the soldiers when Jesus forgave them? Perhaps they were stunned into awe-filled silence, or maybe they fell on their knees and worshipped. Or, better still, they rushed to His cross crying for mercy.

Dr Luke gives us three stark reactions to the glorious magnificence of His forgiveness:

"And they (the soldiers) divided up His clothes by casting lots." (Luke 23:34)

A little later we are told that the soldiers came up and mocked Him (Luke 23:36).

"The people stood watching, and the rulers even sneered at Him." (Luke 23:35)

"One of the criminals who hung there hurled insults at Him…" (Luke 23:39)

We know that the centurion saw something and that one of the criminals "turned to Him", but what about the rest of *them*? ᗐ To offer forgiveness when those who offended us haven't asked for it requires massive courage, but to stick with forgiveness when our offer is greeted with indifference and apathy, demands a fortitude that finds its centre in well-being not winning. ᑎ

No one acknowledged His forgiveness, but He forgave anyway.

He Forgave Them Without Giving His Approval

Jesus was fully aware of what they were doing, even if they weren't, and He knew that all of them were guilty of something.

Pilate was guilty of moral capitulation under political pressure. The Religious were guilty of allowing a personal agenda to eclipse the purity of the Law of God. The soldiers were guilty of apathetic indifference, their consciences seared by an overexposure to brutality. The criminals were guilty of crimes worthy of death under Roman law and Judas was guilty of betraying a friend who only a few nights before had tenderly washed his feet. The disciples were guilty of cowardice and the crowds were guilty of turning a moment of horror into a spectacle. It seems everyone was guilty of something, directly or indirectly related to Jesus that day. From the cross Jesus teaches that it is possible to hate what people do and yet still extend forgiveness to them.

No one acknowledged their guilt and wrongdoing, but He forgave them anyway.

When my recliner broke, I could have spent all my time complaining about the cost, the insurance, the attitude of the company, the fine print and the injustice. But though all of that may have been true, even justifiable, the problem was my recliner remained broken and at some point that had to become the point.

I don't want my life to be defined by the decisions of others, but rather I understand that I have the power within my means to find healing and wholeness, through the grace of God's Word and the power of His Spirit. I can wait for an apology, for a change of mind and for vindication and justice, which may or may not come, or I can get on with the job of allowing the Lord and those He chooses to use, to fix the broken areas of my life and ensure that the moment of pain doesn't win over my God-given purpose. Too many have learned to live with the broken recliner within their hearts, blaming the company and excusing themselves. Don't give in to this temptation for you are better than that and you've been called to more than that.

"Hope deferred makes the heart sick, but a longing fulfilled is a tree of life." (Proverbs 13:12)

Endnotes
1. For more on the power of forgiveness, why not check out The Real F Word, Discovering the Glorious Offence of Forgiveness, New Wine Press, 2009.

Chapter Five
Moving On

"He moved on from there and dug another well..."
(Genesis 26:22)

The last time we looked at Isaac he was on the run, but now, as we meet him again in Genesis 26, he's on the move. Much has changed for the young man in that time. Abraham has died and Isaac has a family of his own, as well as a relationship with the God of his father. This stands out as a significant development in the story of the son of promise. Whereas there is not a single reference to Isaac engaging with God before the death of Abraham, after the passing of the great Patriarch all of that changes.

Isaac prays (his first recorded prayer):

"Isaac prayed to the Lord (Yahweh) on behalf of his wife..." (Genesis 25:21)

The Lord appears and speaks to Isaac twice:

"The Lord (Yahweh) appeared to Isaac and said..." (Genesis 26:2)

"That night the Lord (Yahweh) appeared to him and said..." (Genesis 26:24)

On both occasions when the Lord spoke to Isaac, though

73

He referenced Abraham, there was an explicit promise that He would be with Isaac (v3, 24).

Isaac built an altar (his first):

"Isaac built an altar there and called on the name of the Lord (Yahweh)…" (Genesis 26:25)

In these four significant moments, one glorious fact is common to all, the reference to the Lord by His covenant name. Not once is the Lord referred to using the more generic name of God. Rather, we are given insight into the fact that Isaac is now walking with the Lord and knows Him – not just because his father knew Him, but knows Him for himself. This is further evidence, as already alluded to in chapter 3, that somewhere in his liminal space, Isaac and Yahweh found each other. All seemed to be going well for the son of promise.

"Isaac planted crops in that land and the same year reaped a hundredfold, because the Lord blessed him. The man became rich, and his wealth continued to grow until he became very wealthy." (Genesis 26:12-13)

But even with the backdrop of Isaac's relationship with Yahweh and the subsequent prosperity and blessing he enjoyed, he still had to contend with issues that threatened his life and well-being and he had to learn to move on from them.

Resentment

"He had so many flocks and herds and servants that the Philistines envied him." (Genesis 26:14)

Envy is a bi-product of insecurity and insecurity is always aroused by the prosperity of another. This is exactly the scenario that emerged for Isaac. He was so blessed by the Lord that his prosperity threatened those around him, and they in turn threatened Isaac. Note the nature of their response:

"So all the wells that his father's servants had dug in the time of his father Abraham, the Philistines stopped up, filling them with earth." (Genesis 26:15)

These are not to be confused with the wells already blocked in the Valley of Gerar on Abraham's death, wells that Isaac would later reopen. Rather, these are wells in Gerar itself. The Philistines' resentment of Isaac was so great that they were prepared to block up wells in a region where water was like gold. Such was their envy that they tried to cut off all means by which Isaac could continue to prosper and grow. The word used here is the same as that in Genesis 37:11 where it says that Joseph's brothers were "jealous of him", and we know how that ended. This was envy with zeal.[1]

As Isaac can testify, resentfulness always looks ugly and feels brutal. Whatever the causes of resentment in others, it is never a pleasant thing to experience and whether expressed in critical words or destructive actions, it has a potentially crippling impact on the recipient. The focus of resentment may be your success, your marriage, your family or even your ministry, but its goal is always the same, to diminish its subject and elevate its sender!

We must never fall into the trap of judging the motives of others. That ability is above all our pay grades. But we can discern the culture of any given context by the beliefs and behaviours exhibited by those within it. Over the years I've seen the toxicity of resentment infect families, relationships, churches and ministries. As a child of envy, it often looks the same in different places. Here are some signals of resentment you might recognise.

- Signal #1 – Resentment tolerates but rarely celebrates
- Signal #2 – Resentment expects but rarely empowers

- Signal #3 – Resentment blames but rarely builds
- Signal #4 – Resentment believes the worst but rarely defends the best

We must guard our hearts from becoming the Philistines to an Isaac in our world. Don't allow your own insecurities to nurture envy and resentment that would make you a hindrance rather than a help to those in your world. Isaac carried the blessing of God, but insecurity, envy and resentment saw this only as a threat rather than a glorious opportunity.

We must also guard our hearts from the arrows of resentment fired by others. You may be living in a world that demonstrates one or all of the signals of resentment listed above, but do not let the smallness of others' resentment shrink the world of opportunity before you. Isaac didn't respond to their envious resentment, rather he just kept doing the same thing – and the Lord continued to bless him in spite of their best efforts.

You can rise above resentment!

Rejection

"Then Abimelech said to Isaac, 'Move away from us; you have become too powerful for us.'" (Genesis 26:16)

If the resentful actions of the Philistines were rejection by stealth, then Abimelech comes right out and says it. He wants Isaac gone and asks him to move away on the basis that he has become too powerful. This word *powerful* is also referenced at the beginning of Exodus when speaking of the Hebrews in Egypt. In that context their growth and expansion provoked rejection in the form of enslavement.[2] So the idea here is that Isaac is growing, expanding and increasing, and his influence is starting to disturb Gerar's political and social world. Isaac is rejected on the basis that he is seen as a perceived threat, yet ironically, of all the Patriarchs, he is the most peace loving, not engaging in a single act of violence in his whole life.

Rejection is one of the hardest issues in life to contend with and is a key ingredient in the recipe of brokenness. When someone says, "I/we don't want you", even the most secure human on the planet will find that a test. Even if their reasons for our rejection are justified, it still hurts. But when the reasons are not justified, rejection moves to a whole other level.

As a teenager I was rejected for a job in the Police cadets because of an issue with my eyesight, and I get that. Early attempts at writing a book were rejected by publishers because they didn't think my writing was good enough, and I get that. But twice in my life I've been rejected when I thought I was doing a good job and the facts seemed to support that view. On both occasions the pain I experienced was off the scale and tested the very depths of my being. Even though I considered myself to be a pretty secure person in both identity and call, I found myself asking four challenging questions:

Why Has This Happened?

This had multiple layers to it as you can imagine. I sought an answer from those who rejected me. In the silent moments I asked the Lord for some insight. And, of course, I asked this of myself. As we've seen in the previous chapter, asking and knowing why doesn't ultimately determine our next step, but it was a question I asked nonetheless.

Who Am I?

As the word got out about my situation, one of the most common questions I faced was "What are you going to do now?" It showed me again how much people's value is locked into what they do, and although we can say that the badge doesn't matter, for many people it does. In both these seasons I had to dig into who I was in Christ and find affirmation for my identity again. Though I loved what I did, I knew my doing was only an extension of my being and that it did not define me in the fullest sense. After all, I had taught in many contexts, "We are human beings before doings", but through rejection, like no other experience, this belief, my theology, was thoroughly tested.

What Will People Think?

I'd love to say this didn't bother me, but it did. We try to tell ourselves that the opinions of others don't matter, but in our weakness and brokenness, their views become important and even their silence can be crippling. In my journey through rejection, I was shocked by how many people had an opinion on my life, but I was also saddened by the silence of some I thought were friends. In truth, none of this should matter, but it did and I had to work through the challenge of what people thought about me ... or not!

Where To Next?

Of course, when one is handed one's P45 the question is, *now what?* What a scary question that can be. I was 47 and 49, respectively, when both rejections landed in my lap and although I've always had confidence in the promises of the Lord, rejection seeds those "Will anyone want me now?" sort of questions.

When I was only sixteen years old, the Lord gave me a promise and in all the years since He has never broken it:

"I will instruct you and teach you in the way you should go; I will counsel you and watch over you." (Psalm 32:8)

However, in the brokenness of rejection, I still found myself asking, "Where to next?" Remember, the Lord is not afraid of our questions, but they can hurt us if we get stuck on them.

You can move beyond rejection!

Contention

"But the herdsmen of Gerar quarrelled with Isaac's herdsmen and said, 'The water is ours!' So he named the well Esek..." (Genesis 26:20)

Aside from unblocking his father's wells and renewing the names given to them by Abraham, Isaac also goes to work opening his own wells. He not only benefits from the legacy left by his father, but he builds on it. It is interesting that the locals don't contend with him over Abraham's existing wells, but they do take issue with anything new Isaac wants to do. They are content enough for him to reopen the old, but they have an issue with him opening something new. The basis of their contention with Isaac is, "the water is ours", even though they have no legitimate right or claim to it. After all, it was Isaac's men who dug the well. Their contention, however, is really about containment, because they don't want the man of God to expand any further into "their" territory. If they cannot make him small, they will do all in their power to ensure he won't get any bigger.

Why didn't Isaac fight for this well? He seems to let it go without a struggle and moves on to dig another one. It is hard to know his motivation here, but there is no hint of cowardice or fear in the text. Instead there is an almost casual acceptance that his opponents have seized the rights to the well and Isaac simply moves on.

As I've written already in this book, there is a time to fight and a time to let go. And although letting go looks like cowardice, it can be courage. In letting go we show the courage to leave an issue God's hands and not take it into our own. In letting go we show the courage to believe in a bigger picture that exists above and beyond the moment. In letting go we truly trust that the Lord can work all the details out for us and whatever the short-term loss, we know that there will be a long-term gain.

I love how Solomon puts it:

"In his heart a man plans his course, but the Lord determines his steps."

Later in the same chapter he says,

"The lot is cast into the lap, but its every decision is from the Lord." (Proverbs 16:9, 33)

Do we dare believe this? That in situations that seem beyond our control, the Lord can work it out for His glory and our good? Do we have the courage to let go of the contention and trust the Lord to fight for us? Is it possible to be at such rest that we allow others to take what was ours, knowing the Lord has more for us ahead? Paul thinks so:

"And we know that in all things God works for the good of those who love Him, who have been called according to His purpose." (Romans 8:28)

You can overcome contention!

Accusation

"Then they dug another well, but they quarrelled over that one also; so he named it Sitnah." (Genesis 26:21)

On the surface of it, *Sitnah* looks like a repeat of *Esek*, yet Isaac gives it a different name, which has within it a subtle nuance, pointing perhaps to the fact that something deeper is going on. Though the word means opposition it carries an accusatory aspect to it, thus his opponents are not just contending with Isaac, as before, but now their hostility it barbed with an accusation of some description.

In Ezra 4:6 this same word is used to bring a formal legal complaint to King Xerxes against the people of Judah and Jerusalem.[3] We don't know what this was, but clearly it represents an increase in antagonism, where the language moves from "this is ours" to "you are up to something". *Esek* was a defence of what they believed was theirs, but *Sitnah* was an attack on Isaac himself, perhaps in an attempt to discredit him before his men or the wider community. Whatever the accusation, they used it in an attempt to force Isaac to move on.

Christmas 2016 was a season of mixed emotions for me. It was a delight to have all the family around the dinner table as we celebrated a Christmas of freedom with Simeon. However, it was also the end of a gruelling six months for Dawn and myself in which, on top of Simeon's court case, I had been accused of certain things (none of them immoral or illegal), which ultimately cost me my job. From June of that year, things were said to me and about me that I struggled to process; things that in thirty years of ministry I'd never been accused of before. As you might imagine, the pain was immense, but a side-effect I didn't expect was the impact the accusations had on my confidence. I've always loved teaching and preaching, but I found myself having to work hard to motivate myself to do it. Not because I didn't love the churches I was ministering in, or appreciated the privilege of the opportunities I was given, but because of how I felt about myself. How could I stand up and preach God's Word with these accusations on the table? Could I minister effectively when I had been sacked from my job? Why would anyone want to listen to me when this had happened?

I'm grateful for the patience of my wife, Dawn, who walked with me every step of the way and I'm thankful for Simon Jarvis who kept reassuring me I'd be okay, as well as numerous friends and church leaders who welcomed me to their churches and pulpits, affirming me in the process. These, coupled with the comfort of the Lord's presence and the power of His Word, sustained me in and beyond my *Sitnah*. Without them, I may have given up at that well.

You can survive accusation!

Note Isaac's reaction to the contention that is erupting all around him:

"He moved on from there..."

If that's all the text said, then we might think that Isaac is slipping into old ways and going for another run. However, Isaac isn't running from anything or anyone, rather he's moving *to* something:

"...and dug another well..." (Genesis 26:22)

What is holding him in his time of resentment, rejection, contention and accusation, and what is it that is helping him move on?

The clue is given to us earlier in the text, when the Lord appears to him and speaks to him. Maybe, the strength of the word from the Lord is an indication not only of Isaac's destiny, but of the trial he is about to go through. When the Lord speaks He gives Isaac three (by implication four) glorious "I wills".

- *"...I will be with you and (I will) bless you."* (v3)
- *"For to you and your descendants I will give all these lands..."* (v3)

- *"I will make your descendants as numerous as the stars in the sky..."* (v4)

Note, each of these "I wills" potentially relates to the areas of challenge Isaac has experienced.

I will be with you – Rejection
I will bless you – Resentment
I will give you all these lands – Contention (this is ours)
I will make your descendants numerous – Accusation (legal dispute)

Isaac didn't move on because he was afraid or weak. In fact, there is no reference to any of these emotions in the account. Rather, he moved on because he was secure, held by the word the Lord had given to him before these events occurred. What a contrast to chapter 22 and the events of Moriah, where Isaac disappears from the story, drifting without any personal revelation of his own. Now we see a different picture altogether: of a man so secure in the promise that he's able to rise above resentment, move beyond rejection, overcome contention and survive accusation. But even with the word, Isaac still had to journey through each trial, each with the potential to inflict pain and break his resolve. But this time, he kept moving. Isaac teaches us that when we are secure, we can move on!

Look at what he moves on to:

"He moved on from there and dug another well, and no one quarrelled over it. He named it Rehoboth, saying, 'Now the Lord (Yahweh) has given us room and we will flourish in the land.'" (Genesis 26:22)

Isaac travelled from resentment, rejection, contention and

accusation to a place of expansion because he kept moving and refused to get stuck at any stage of this treacherous journey. Had Isaac reacted to resentment he would never have made it to *Rehoboth*. Had he fought rejection, he would not have made it to *Rehoboth*. Had he given in to contention and cracked under accusation, he would never have made it to *Rehoboth*. He made it because he kept moving, and he kept moving because he had the word of the Lord inside him.

There is a *Rehoboth* waiting for you, a place of increase and blessing, a place of prosperity and expansion, but you must keep moving and not get trapped in the cul-de-sac of self-justification. Don't allow the resentment of others to hold you, or the rejection of people to cripple you. Don't give contention permission to derail you or cruel accusations to bind you. Go back to the "I wills" the Lord gave you, dust down His promises and once again speak them over the wells of *Esek* and *Sitnah* so that you can live in the blessing of *Rehoboth*.

But notice one final thing. From *Rehoboth* Isaac entered into a whole new season of increase, expansion and influence. He moved to a new place (v23), had a fresh encounter with the Lord (v24), built his first altar (v25) and dug yet another well (v25). In between digging the well and naming it, Isaac receives a visit from Abimelech in which his former adversary asks for the establishment of a treaty, so the two men can live in peace. Abimelech saw that the Lord was with Isaac and concluded, with the Lord's help, that he would only continue to increase and expand, so he wanted to protect his own interests by sealing an agreement. The text concludes,

"Early the next morning the men swore an oath to each other. Then Isaac sent them on their way, and they left him in peace." (Genesis 26:31)

As if to mark the event, the well Isaac's servants had previously dug produced water on the day Abimelech left – a sign of the Lord's blessing on His servant. Isaac named the well *Shibah*, which in this context most likely points to the oath he had just established.[4] Though Abraham had also dug a well in what became know as Beersheba, the text is clear that this well was Isaac's, not his father's. Hence the significance of the moment in which a well is dug and named by Isaac to celebrate the treaty signed with Abimelech, establishing him as a key personality in the land of promise. The fourth well represents a hugely significant moment for Isaac. He's moved from the place of blessing, *Rehoboth,* to a place of building, *Shibah*. And with an oath now established, a people can now be built.

The Lord not only wants to take you to a place of blessing, but even beyond that, to a place where He can build something through you. So many see Rehoboth as the end because the goal is blessing, but I believe the Lord wants us to push beyond need, or the satisfaction of blessing in itself, to a place where that blessing can be used to establish something for His glory in His world, through our lives. The trials of resentment, rejection, contention and accusation are not to stop us getting to *Rehoboth*, but to prevent us getting to *Shibah*, the well of oath, from which we can influence our "Abimelech" and impact the nations of our world. Don't give up, keep moving!

Endnotes
1. Jealous and zealous - קָנָא (qā·nā('))
2. See Exodus 1:7 & 20 - עָצַם ('ā·ṣăm)
3. שִׂטְנָה (śiṭ·nā(h)) - From the same root we get the word satan, the accuser.
4. Genesis 21:31-32 - The place where Abraham made an agreement with Abimelech was called Beersheba relating perhaps to the seven ewe lambs given by Abraham as an affirmation that he had dug the well there. The word can point to seven or oath.

Chapter Six
From Disappointed to Disappointment

"Hope deferred makes the heart sick,
but a longing fulfilled is a tree of life."
(Proverbs 13:12)

If ever there was a picture of disappointment, Luke 24:13-35 captures it for us beautifully. The chapter explodes into life with the magnificence of the resurrection of Jesus and ends with the glory of His ascension, but sandwiched in between is the image of two ordinary disciples of Jesus struggling to come to terms with the events they've just experienced. The reality of their disappointment saturates the early part of the story as they explain to the uninformed stranger who joins them,

"...we had hoped that he was the one..." (Luke 24:21)

For them, disappointed had now become disappointment. The *disappointed of the cross* had now become in them, the *disappointment of defeat* as they headed home to Emmaus, seven miles in the wrong direction. The *event* they witnessed had now become their *experience,* and the *crisis* of the loss of Jesus now framed the *choice* for their abandonment of Jerusalem and His cause.

It seems like a natural progression that something that

disappointed me would develop into a disappointment for me, but as I've discovered on my journey through brokenness, these are two separate (if similar) things, joined only by my decision to bring them together. I've discovered that disappointed is an *event*, whereas disappointment is an *experience*. The former is a moment of crisis, but the latter is lived as a choice.

So, my team lose in the cup final – that is disappointed. But then I burn my scarf and vow never watch them play again – that is disappointment. The dog chews my favourite shoes – that is disappointed. Selling the dog on eBay as a consequence – that's disappointment. Someone lets me down – that's disappointed. But now nobody can be trusted – that's disappointment. "Lord, why has this happened to me?" – that is disappointed. But, "Lord, I'm out and I'm done with serving you and your Church" – that is disappointment. Disappointed happens to everybody, but disappointment is a choice we make.

We have an enemy who wants us to live in disappointment because it is such a disabling and destructive place. Like the two on the road, it will rob us of our joy, explain away the promises of God, empty us of our strength and take us in the wrong direction. Disappointment is a powerful foe. If we allow it to take up residence in our hearts it will rule us without compassion, until every spark of hope and life has gone. Job, who wrestled with the darkness of his own brokenness, summarised it this way:

"My spirit is broken, my days are cut short, the grave awaits me." (Job 17:1)

When Job spoke of a broken spirit, the implication is of a "corrupted, disturbed and troubled spirit". However, his despair was not because of his circumstances, although these were truly horrific at times, it emerged from the brokenness he felt in his spirit. His heart, which was once pure with hope and faith, was now "disturbed" because of the inroads hopelessness had been allowed to make into it. A moment of disappointed had now become a mind-set of disappointment!

I would love to tell you that in my own journey the disappointed moments remained just that, but on too many occasions I found myself giving in to the pain, and permitting the moment to grow into something much bigger. There were times when I allowed events to determine my experience and words spoken by others to become the framework of my thinking. Without exception, every time I permitted disappointed to become disappointment, I lost my way, and slipped a little further into the darkness.

This expressed itself in my relationship with my son. I found it an almost relentless battle not to allow the "disappointed" of the event that put us all in harm's way to become disappointment *with him*. Dawn and I have been blessed with three amazing children, each of them so different and all of them talented. We have tried to love and support each one of them and hopefully allowed them to move into being the person they were designed by God to be. But Simeon's ordeal (and ours with him) tested me to the very depths of my soul. Though I never wavered in my love for my son, there were times when I didn't like him very much. I hated the depression that gripped him, I was freaked out by the self-harming, and there were moments when I was angry at the pressure this brought to bear on the family. It felt like the devil was trying to kill us, and that sense of despair only fed the disappointment in my soul.

In this season, I knew disappointed had become disappointment, because it manifested itself in four powerful and potentially destructive ways.

Disappointment Deflates

Have you ever had a slow puncture? It's a puncture, so it is serious, but because it's slow, we might have a tendency to not treat it with the seriousness it deserves. With a normal puncture we would replace or repair the tyre immediately and get it fixed, but with a slow puncture, we are tempted to make do until we get around to it. So when it goes down we pump it up, drive to our destination, then pump it up again, do another bit of driving and pump it up yet again. As long as the hole doesn't get any bigger, we'll be fine. However, if we're not careful, we learn to live with something that is both broken and dangerous; because we can pump it up, we make do.

Disappointment is like a slow puncture to the soul, doing something to us on the inside that, if not attended to, leaks life and energy, taking more and more work to pump it up. Heartache that crushes the spirit means we have to work harder and harder on the outside, smiling, working, serving and giving, all while we're leaking with the pain that has punctured our soul.

The two on the road to Emmaus were deflated at worst or leaking at best:

"They stood still, their faces downcast." (Luke 24:17)

The word translated "downcast" here is *skuthrōpós* and carries the meaning of grimness or sternness, and of sadness that affects the countenance. This is exactly Solomon's idea when he says,

"A happy heart makes the face cheerful, but heartache crushes the spirit." (Proverbs 15:13)

For Solomon, our inner world informs our outer disposition. Of course, every one of us has had to learn to hide the pain of our hearts in front of our children, employees or church members, but in this unscripted and unguarded moment, the two don't disguise how they really feel.

Don't keep pumping; it's time to get the tyre repaired and that requires both honesty and humility. We need honesty to admit we have a puncture and humility to find the means to get it fixed. The puncture doesn't mean we are weak or feeble, it just means we're human.

Disappointment Distorts

When I was in Sunday School as a child, my teacher taught me that Job never questioned God and that through all his trials he remained faithful and true ... and then I read the book for myself! Though Job ultimately journeys through the darkest of valleys, he certainly had a few interesting moments within it and his discourse, captured in chapters 16 and 17, is filled with words so honest and, at times, brutal, that it might have great pastors shifting in their seats:

- *"Surely, O God, You have worn me out."* (16:7)
- *"... You have devastated my entire household."* (16:7)
- *"You have bound me..."* (16:8)
- *"God ... gnashes His teeth at me..."* (16:9)
- *"God has turned me over to evil men..."* (16:11)
- *"Again and again He bursts upon me; He rushes at me like a warrior."* (16:14)
- *"God has made me a byword to everyone..."* (17:6)

Though Job felt this to be true, it actually wasn't true. His pain and his disappointment had distorted his view of God – the God who had previously blessed him and made him a man of means and influence. When Job opens his mouth, this is not truth speaking, this is disappointment speaking.

I have learned the principle that "we see the world as we are, not as it is". You and I see the world through the dominant "lens" inside us – whether that's to do with colour, gender, culture, experience or creed. Whatever we believe frames what we see and that is why disappointment is so destructive. Disappointment can convince us of a reality that doesn't actually exist; that people are against us when they are not; that God hates us when He doesn't. It becomes a stronghold in our thinking, which when reinforced by our pain becomes very difficult to break.

When Jesus joined the two on the road, He asked them what they were talking about. They were amazed that He didn't know. Thinking He was a stranger, they spoke from the heart in an unguarded, unscripted moment. So what came out next was what they truly believed:

"He was a prophet, powerful in word and deed before God and all the people... but we had hoped he was the one who was going to redeem Israel ... In addition, some of our women amazed us." (Luke 24:19-24)

Look at their words carefully. As we read what they said, it is also striking to see what they didn't say. They don't declare Jesus emphatically as the Christ, the Son of the Living God. They don't see Him as the Saviour and they certainly don't believe He has or will rise from the dead, or else they would not have left the city. Everything they heard before, all the words He spoke to them and the promise of resurrection, dissipated into the fog of despair and the confusion of disappointment. They said what they saw, and even though Jesus was standing right in front of them, their disappointment framed a world and a future in which He did not exist.

Disappointment Distracts

Two gorgeous Sausage dogs currently make up part of our family, namely Pepperoni and Salami. They have brought great joy to us, as well as many puppies (ten and counting) and we love walking them in the woods. Though small, they can travel far. However, when out walking with them we have to be constantly on the lookout for the sort of distractions that will send our little hounds into a delirious pursuit. Yes, I'm talking about squirrels and rabbits. Pep and Sal could be walking along, happily minding their own business, when suddenly they catch a glimpse of something and they are off. I've even seen Sal trying to climb a tree while a squirrel looked down on her mockingly. Once distracted it's hard to get them back and we're just grateful for extendable leads!

My Sausage dogs aren't alone. Asaph found himself distracted when he said,

"Surely God is good to Israel, to those who are pure in heart. But as for me, my feet had almost slipped; I had nearly lost my foothold. For I envied the arrogant when I saw the prosperity of the wicked." (Psalm 73:1-3)

Note that the psalm starts off with a great confession, but almost immediately, Asaph is distracted by something he saw. His disappointed soon became disappointment and so dominated his vision that it eclipsed his view of God and took him in a direction that almost destroyed him, admitting,

"When my heart was grieved and my spirit embittered, I was senseless and ignorant; I was a brute beast before You." (v21-22)

In my own journey I discovered that disappointment distracted me in such a way, that at times it was all I could see. I was reminded again of the truth that "we follow our focus". My body follows where my eyes lead and if my eyes are on the pain, then that's the tree I'm going to be barking up, no matter who or what is around me. Disappointment can distract us from the Lord, His Word, our family, the good things we already have in our lives, and our purpose. When the squirrel of disappointment is running around, it's hard to see anything else. And that's the tragedy: while pursuing the distraction we're missing out on living.

When Jesus joined the two, they were heading in the wrong direction, destination Emmaus. This is the only time in the whole of the Bible this little village is mentioned, and the only reason we have note of it here is because it's the wrong direction. Disappointment had so distracted these two disciples (possibly man and wife, though we assume they were both men) that they are heading for home, seven miles from the epicentre of Jerusalem where they had been encouraged to stay. So great was their distraction that it never even crossed their minds that the stranger on the road with them might be the One they had hoped for. For these two broken hearts, home was the only thing on their minds.

Disappointment Infects

Nits. The very mention of the word will probably start you scratching, so my apologies. Oh, the times Dawn had to get the nit comb out for our children because they came home from school with much more than their homework. We would send them out clean, washed and scrubbed for the day, and yet I can't remember how many times they came back with little friends in their hair. Relatively close contact with a carrier of the dreaded head louse ensured we too got to enjoy their blessing. But their end came quickly as Dawn got to work with her comb – an experience that neither of my daughters enjoyed.

David, the greatest king Israel ever had, almost didn't get to be king because of the infectious nature of disappointment. He and his men had been out on a raiding party and when they returned someone had raided the camp and taken everything – their wives, children and possessions. The text starkly reveals,

"David was greatly distressed because the men were talking of stoning him; each one bitter in spirit because of his sons and daughters." (1 Samuel 30:6)

Ironically, David had wept with them earlier (v4), but something had happened *between* his men that caused them to think of turning on him, even though it was not his fault. The text gives us the answer that his men had become "bitter in spirit" and in talking together, they fed off each other, infecting each other with their own pain and brokenness.

We don't like to think of disappointment being infectious, but it is and that's why it must be fought. It has the power to infect a marriage, a family, a business and a church, if we let it, as one person's pain feeds on the other. Talking together is good, but we must beware of what we are talking about, for one conversation can challenge the bitterness, whilst another can encourage it.

The two on the road were undoubtedly rehearsing the pain and disappointment they felt. Dr Luke tells us,

"They were talking with each other about everything that had happened." (Luke 24:14)

It is interesting that when Jesus joined them He wanted to know what they were talking about, and by asking, interrupted their council of pity. What is fascinating is that once they tell Him their thoughts, He then steps into their conversation and drives it forward with a different agenda, one centred on Moses and the Prophets; a conversation during which, they later confessed, their hearts were caused to "burn within them" (v32). As they talked alone, their conversation fed the pain and broken heartedness they felt. But as they talked with Him, without knowing who He was, His words started to bring healing to their hearts.

The turning point of their story, of course, is not when the two got up to return to Jerusalem (v33), but when Jesus joined them on the road to Emmaus. However, before we see how He helped them, there is at the heart of this story and wider passage, a slightly disturbing paradox that cannot be ignored. Luke 24 is full of openings. The chapter begins with an open grave and ends with an open heaven, but in between these two world-changing bookends, there are three statements of opening:

- *"Then their eyes were opened and they recognised Him..."*[1] (v31)
- *"...opened the Scriptures to us?"* (v32)
- *"Then He opened their minds so they could understand the Scriptures."* (v45)

In each case there are three common factors.

Firstly, the word used for "opening" is the same on each occasion, pointing to exactly the same idea each time. The word is *dianoígō*, meaning "to open what was closed before", "to open as the firstborn opens the womb". The idea in this context is to see something by revelation, as if for the first time.

Secondly, someone is doing the opening, external to the subject being opened – the implication being that this is not something the disciples are doing, but rather something being done to and for them.

Thirdly, every time something is opened there is a supernatural response.

- When their eyes are opened, they *recognised* Him
- When the Scriptures were opened, their hearts *burned* within them
- When their minds were opened, they *understood* the Scriptures

Set this against the statement recorded for us in verse 16:

"But they were kept from recognising Him."

The word translated "kept" makes it clear that in the same way their eyes were opened by an external action, so in this case they were kept from recognising Jesus by a similar action. In the passage where eyes, minds and Scriptures are opened, someone kept the eyes of the two shut so they did not "see" the stranger who walked with them on the road. How can this be? Why would the Lord do such a thing? Why didn't Jesus just simply reveal Himself immediately to them and put them out of their misery? Why did He remain hidden all the way to Emmaus?

There are times on our journey when we cannot see, hear or feel the Lord. Theologically we know He is with us, because His word declares this truth, but there are moments when, outside of that fact, nothing else seems to point to His presence. This has happened to every serious follower of Jesus at least once in his/her life and it may be happening to you now. When we can't see, feel or hear Him, our reactions and responses reveal our heart and show us what is truly inside us. As followers of Jesus we like to think that we believe all the right stuff, but it is not until we are squeezed, put under pressure or simply left to our own devices that we find out what we truly believe. With Jesus in the room, surrounded by the other disciples, these two on the road would have looked and sounded like hard-core followers. But now that there's no sign of Jesus and the other disciples are somewhere back in Jerusalem, true belief emerges in the presence of the hidden stranger.

I believe Dr Luke suggests three reasons in the text why they may have been kept from recognising Him.

Jesus Wanted To Hear What They Would Say

As a youngster I often went to my granny's house after school, while I waited for my mum to come home from work. My granny Bailie (my mum's mum) had a contraption in her garden called a mangle. People of a certain age may need to Google that. Essentially it was a way of squeezing the water out of newly washed clothes by passing them between two enamel rollers. However, as a child I wondered what else would go through the mangle and yes, you guessed it, all sorts of insects and bugs found their way to heaven via my granny's mangle, worms making the most mess (I have asked for forgiveness for these crimes against bugdom). I discovered that if something is squeezed hard enough, what is inside it comes out!

Jesus' question "What things?" (v19) provoked an unscripted and unguarded response and such answers are usually the truth … at least for us! The death of Jesus and the painful post-crucifixion silence had squeezed these faithful disciples hard, until what was really inside them came out. Am I suggesting that the Lord is cruel to His children and that He's playing some sort of sadistic game with our lives? No, not at all. But there are moments, even when disappointed, when He will step back and say nothing, to hear what we will say.

Jesus Wanted To See Where They Would Go

I get the joy of travelling all over the country to preach and teach the Word of God, so I'm grateful for my Satnav (Sally, as already introduced). When I climb into my car at the end of ministering at a church and switch on my Satnav, a home screen appears that has on it a picture of a little house. That's my home button. As soon as I hit that, the Satnav springs into action, calculating the fastest way to get me home. It's a wonderful feeling. Sometimes I'll turn it on and hit the home button even though I know the way home! Home is my place of comfort, safety, security, acceptance and love. Love is where everything makes sense.

When the disciples were put through the mangle of seeing Jesus tortured and executed, I'm sure at that moment, everyone wanted to hit the home button. But that's why Jesus had tried to prepare them for this trauma – so that they wouldn't head home, but stay where He wanted them to be. The two couldn't take it anymore and even though rumours started to emerge that Jesus wasn't in His grave, they switched on the Satnav and headed for home. What's lovely is that Jesus joined them on their journey and even though they were heading in the wrong direction, He walked all the way to Emmaus with them. But why? So that eventually He would get the chance to change their home button.

Jesus Wanted To Test What They Would Do

A defining moment of the journey comes as they reach their home in Emmaus. The text tells us,

"Jesus acted as if He were going further." (v28)

Why this apparent pretence? Jesus wanted to test if what they were feeling in their hearts would translate into action and their response is striking:

"But they urged Him strongly, 'Stay with us...'" (v29)

Now it might be suggested that was just two good Jewish people offering another Jewish person basic hospitality, and for sure, this cannot be discounted. But the text suggests something deeper is happening. Remember, as He opened the Scriptures, their hearts were burning inside them, so by the time He's ready to leave, they "urge Him strongly" to stay. They verbally grab Him and pull Him into their home, doing everything but physically restraining Him. It's this moment of desperation and passion that opened the door into their home, and which ultimately allowed Him to open their eyes. With opened eyes, their disappointment vanished and they returned at once to Jerusalem echoing the confession:

"It is true! The Lord has risen..." (v34)

There were many times in the journey through the dark valley of brokenness, when I couldn't see Him, feel Him or hear Him. When disappointed morphed into disappointment and so gripped my soul that I found myself deflated and empty. In this trial of faith, when my Master remained "hidden" from me, I have come to believe He wanted to hear what I would say, see where I would go, and test what I would do. Sometimes I passed the test, but other times I didn't do so well. The enemy tried to drive a wedge between myself and my son, hoping that the moment of disappointed would become a mind-set of disappointment ... and it almost worked. I gave in to the pain and the hurt and heard my mind rehearse unthinkable thoughts. But in it all, the Lord walked with me and like the two on the road, there was a day when in desperation I cried out to Him and pleaded, "Stay with me." In that moment, as I sobbed in His presence, He spoke to me, opening the Scriptures and the eyes of my understanding to see something beyond the disappointment. Through His promise He renewed my faith and through His grace He restored my love. I love my son, but in my own disappointment I almost lost him by allowing him to become a disappointment to me.

In February 2017, Simeon turned 20 and we celebrated a wonderful birthday with him. However, I had deep words in my heart I needed to say to him, words of love, redemption and hope and the only way I found to frame them properly was in a letter to him. With his kind permission you can read what I wrote:

"Dearest Shim,

Happy 20th birthday my son. And I am so happy that we are celebrating with you as a free man. This time last year I would have given anything for you to be a free man today, and by God's grace, our prayers have been heard and He has given you a second chance, an opportunity for a new beginning.

I hope you like your gift. We got you a watch because we want to stand with you and believe that this is your time; a new day, a moment of hope and possibility that you can grasp and make the most of. I know that the last 18 months have been horrible, but you have been given a gift to move on, move forward and avenge the pain of the past with a life well lived.

The two psalms that the Lord gave me for you through the process of the trial were 124 and 34, the two I'll have on my tattoo. I wanted to remind you of the words contained in them:

Praise be to the Lord, who has not let us be torn by their teeth.
We have escaped like a bird out of the fowler's snare;

The snare has been broken, and we have escaped.
Our help is in the name of the Lord, the Maker of heaven and earth.

I believe the Lord broke the snare that held us all and set us free. That week in court we saw His hand manoeuvre the circumstances to create the moment of your freedom. You and I know this to be true.

A righteous man may have many troubles, but the Lord delivers him from them all; He protects all his bones, not one of them will be broken.

By 'bones' the Lord told me this meant you – that you, 'my bone', would not be broken; that you would not be lost. He was true to His word and you have not been lost to me.

The Lord has also told me that you will be called *Shuvael*, which means 'captive (or returned) of God'. The Lord told me you would return; you would be His captive. I speak this word over you every day, that *Shimon Yochanan* will be *Shuvael*. Perhaps one day this will be another of my (or your) tattoos! The tears I cried in the court that day were not simply of relief that you were found not guilty, but that this was part of the fulfilment of the Lord's promise to me for you. This was the 'first stage' of His salvation of you, literally saving you from jail, and that one day, He will redeem your heart and life, and cause you to be the man you were made to be.

I love you my son. When you were cooking in your mother's womb, a trusted friend came to me in a prayer meeting. He didn't know your mother was pregnant and asked me if she was. When I told him she was, he told me that God has spoken to him about you. He told me that Dawn would have a boy and that one day he would fulfil the things that I could not. I don't fully know what this means, but I do know it will demand great things of you one day; things beyond your own strength and ability; things that can only happen when your life is placed firmly in the hands of our Lord.

When I wrote the book *Hope*, I dedicated it to you. The dedication reads,

Simeon John Carey
Number One Son
Your destiny is not to live in my shadow but to create your own.
You have a zeal for life and a sensitive heart. Hold on to both.
In the challenges which lie ahead, may hope be your constant companion.
I love you.
His children will be mighty in the land;
the generation of the upright will be blessed.
(Psalm 112:2)

How prophetic those words have turned out to be and, I believe, will continue to be. I pray that hope will live in your heart and help transform your thinking about yourself, the Lord and your world. There is so much within you that the Lord has designed and wants to use, but you have an enemy who wants to destroy you, to eradicate the image and glory of God within you.

My prayer is that you will see yourself as the Lord made you. That one day you will love yourself as He sees you; that you will no longer feel the need to cut or injure your own body. I love you, but I hate the cuts and it breaks my heart to see you do this to yourself. Every cut, cuts my heart and every scar I carry within. In truth, I struggle to cope with the cutting … thank God for your wonderful mother.

May you have an amazing birthday. So much lies ahead of you. So much is now behind you. Somebody once said, 'There are two great days in our life, the day we were born and the day we discovered why.' May you be able to celebrate the day you were born, the day you brought so much joy and happiness into our lives, and may you discover the reason you were born – the purpose for which you were made by God and the destiny that He has placed within your soul! I love you. I have always loved you. I will always love you.

Happy birthday.
Dad."

* * *

Don't let disappointed become disappointment and rob you of your family or your destiny. He is with you and He is for you.

> *"Then you will know that I am the Lord;*
> *those who hope in Me will not be disappointed."*
> (Isaiah 49:23)

Chapter Seven
Pressed And Poured

"Not as I will, but as You will."
(Matthew 26:39)

The doctor looked straight at me and without flinching or showing any emotion said, "Your father has 3-6 months to live. He'll be doing well to see Christmas." It was August 2013 and we were enjoying a holiday together on the north coast of Northern Ireland. My mum and dad were both staying with us in the holiday let, so we took them back down to Belfast to see the consultant who was going to give us the results of dad's tests. He hadn't been well for a while, but he had placed his own needs on the back burner, while the family worked through and processed the loss of my brother Alex, who passed away in May 2013. The doctor's words bounced around in my head as I sat alone with him, my parents having left the room while we talked.

As I approached the door to leave, I hesitated. I knew when I walked out my parents would want to know what the doctor had said and my face would tell them everything before words were spoken. I composed myself, took a deep breath and opened the door. The first face I saw was my father's, as he looked straight at me. I smiled at him and he smiled back. I'll never forget his words to me: "Everything alright son?"

A lump of emotion threatened to choke me as I managed to find some words, "Yes pop, just had a wee chat to the doctor. Do you fancy a wee cup of tea?" My mum knew what I could not say, but smiled and said nothing. We would talk and cry later. My dad took my arm as we walked slowly towards the café and in that touch of tenderness I fought back the thoughts that my hero was dying and that moments like these would soon only be memories.

My dad didn't want to know what the doctor said or what the prognosis was, so the whole family made a decision not to tell him, but just to love him. While on holiday we all managed our emotions when he was in the room, but everything I did with him had a tinge of sadness as I realised it might be the last time we did this together. However, there was a moment on holiday I shall never forget. My mum and dad had a bedroom downstairs beside the kitchen and one morning as I headed in to prepare some breakfast I noticed their bedroom door was slightly open. I looked through to make sure they were okay and I saw my father, already up and dressed, sitting on the sofa beside the bed with his Bible in his hand, reading and praying.

I watched, in silent awe, the man (who I suspect knew he was dying but didn't want to know how or when) sitting with the greatest Book in the universe in his hands, worshipping the Lord he had followed since his conversion when he was ten-years-old. Without making a noise I reached for my phone and took a picture of that moment, capturing a glimpse of holy rest. No one was looking, no lights were on him, he wasn't in front of his congregation and there was no band helping to create an atmosphere. It was just him, the Book and His Lord.

My father now faced death as he had lived his life – in Christ!

Gethsemane is the place where Jesus wrestled with the reality that He was going to die. All four Gospel writers include it in their accounts, and through the lens of these witnesses the paradox and intensity of His experience is captured for us, as Jesus processed His darkest valley and looked to heaven for the light of hope.[1] *Gethsemane* means "olive press"[2] and surely it cannot be a coincidence that Jesus, our Saviour, experienced one of His greatest moments of *pressing* in a place called *olive press*. Though the torture to come, climaxing in the crucifixion, heaped physical brutality on Jesus, Gethsemane was a spiritual, psychological and emotional press that squeezed every part of who He was so relentlessly that Dr Luke tells us "…His sweat was like drops of blood falling to the ground" and that an angel appeared to Him and "…strengthened Him" (Luke 22:43-44). Both Matthew and Mark give us Jesus' own conclusion on His condition as He entered the press:

"My soul is overwhelmed with sorrow to the point of death." (Matthew 26:38; Mark 14:34)

If the cross was where humanity's redemption was paid, the olive press was where it was secured. The decisions made in that garden, under the most severe and extreme circumstances, ensured that humanity had a hope and a future. For that night, Jesus expressed faith that found its ultimate demonstration on the cross.

In 2012 I had the privilege of visiting Israel for the second time. It's an amazing country on many levels and is worth being on any bucket list. For me it was the contextualisation of the Bible that made it so exciting, as dots connected and I saw things in three dimensions that reading and study alone couldn't provide. One such experience was seeing a re-creation

107

of a 1ˢᵗ Century olive press and having some of the process explained to us. Once harvested, the olives were washed and crushed to remove the pits (which included the seeds), then the remaining pulp was placed in woven bags or baskets and slowly pressed by a large, weighted crushing stone. The oil then ran into a surrounding channel and from there into a reservoir where it was allowed to settle and separate. As our guide continued to explain the process, he said something that struck me regarding the pressing process: that it was important to press the olive but not crush the pit, because the pit can release bitterness into the oil.[3]

Could this be what's happening to Jesus in Gethsemane? What's clear is that the Father is not trying to crush or destroy the life of His Son in the olive press, but rather, ensure that pure oil will be released from Him as the pressure of the moment presses Him. As we put the events of Gethsemane together, we can see that Jesus experienced four dramatic pressings, which involved the Father, His disciples, His betrayer and the crowd. On their own, each of these would be difficult enough, but rolled together in the space of a few hours, they created an episode that might potentially crush Jesus (His life) rather than press Him (His oil). As Jesus was *pressed*, the Father wanted His oil and undoubtedly the devil wanted His seed, but it was the response of Jesus that determined whether blessing or bitterness flowed from the garden.[4]

The Oil Of Submission

At the heart of Gethsemane is a relationship between a Son and His Father and it's to the Father that the Son turns in His time of need:

"My Father, if it is possible, may this cup be taken from Me." (Matthew 26:39)

"Abba, Father, everything is possible for you. Take this cup from Me." (Mark 14:36)

"Father, if you are willing, take this cup from Me..." (Luke 22:42)

Just as Father is the first recorded word out of Jesus' mouth on the cross, so in prayer in the garden, His Father finds pre-eminence. In the midst of His crisis Jesus looks up to the "Maker of heaven and earth", to the One who is able to deliver Him. He knows that only His Father can either provide an exit out of the press or the power to stay within it, and that's why He prays. We know that Jesus prayed three times, but Matthew gives us most of the detail. His first prayer is recorded in Matthew 26:39 as seen above, then His second prayer is in verse 42:

"My Father, if it is not possible for this cup to be taken away unless I drink it, may Your will be done."

We don't have the detail of the third prayer from any of the Gospels, but Matthew informs us:

"So He left them and went away once more and prayed a third time, saying the same thing." (v44)

What's striking is that though Jesus prayed, the Father did not answer. There is no verbal response to any of the three requests offered up in the garden. The Father who spoke to Him at His baptism, His transfiguration and after His entry into Jerusalem, now remained silent. No words come from heaven to encourage Jesus as He looked for guidance. Instead He is confronted with absolute silence.

So what is His response?

"Yet not as I will, but as You will." (Matthew 26:39)

"...may Your will be done." (Matthew 26:42)

When presented with silence, Jesus submitted to the Father. He did not argue, fight or complain at what was placed before Him. Instead, He drank the cup. At that moment, Jesus did not simply say yes to the purpose of the cross, but to the Father Himself; to someone He loved. When pressed, the oil of submission flowed.

Saying yes to the Father when we neither like nor understand the cup that is placed before us, is the primary decision that allows the oil of life to flow and prevent the bitterness of death taking hold of our souls. We are not saying yes to the cup, for who in their right mind would want to drink a cup like that? But rather we are saying yes to Him. No one would say yes to a cross, or betrayal, or pain or brokenness, and that is not what the Father asks of us. But rather, when pressed, He asks us to trust Him and submit to Him, even when silence is the only thing we can hear.

Paul knew about the pressure of the press, but I love how he framed it:

"... genuine, yet regarded as imposters; known, yet regarded as unknown; dying, and yet we live on; beaten, and yet not killed; sorrowful, yet always rejoicing; having nothing, and yet possessing everything." (2 Corinthians 6:8-10)

Note how he changed the force of the word *yet*. In the first two phrases it is working against him, but in the last four phrases he makes *yet* work for him. I can't help but hear the echo of Habakkuk in Paul's *yet*, when he defiantly declares:

"Though the fig-tree does not bud and there are no grapes on the vines, though the olive crop fails and the fields produce no food, though there are no sheep in the pen and no cattle in the stalls, yet I will rejoice in the Lord, I will be joyful in God my Saviour." (Habakkuk 3:17-18)

Habakkuk did not rejoice in the bitterness of the cup, because earlier he had asked the Lord to explain what was going on, but rather, he came to the place where, even if he had to drink the cup, he would do so because he trusted the Lord who "handed it to him".

Don't look at the cup, look at the face of the Father. If we look at the cup, we'll never drink it, and even if we do, we'll resent it. Either way, bitterness will replace blessing and the press will take our seed rather than release our oil. Say yes to Him and the cup will taste different!

The Oil Of Strength

Dr Luke tells us that the disciples who were with Jesus in the garden were, *"...exhausted from sorrow..."* (Luke 22:45), while Mark and Matthew record the words of Jesus when He said,

"The spirit is willing, but the body is weak." (Mark 14:38; Matthew 26:41).

Maybe that explains why they could not keep their eyes open through this difficult night – a fact that seemed to disappoint Jesus. His main request to His friends that night is captured by Matthew:

"Stay here and keep watch with Me." (Matthew 26:38)

"Could you men not keep watch with me for one hour?" (v40)

But it is the final comment that shows how alone Jesus must have felt:

"When He came back again (for a second time), He again found them sleeping, because their eyes were heavy. So He left them and went away once more and prayed the third time..." (v43-44)

Leaving them was not just an act of mercy from a compassionate Master on His young, weary disciples – it was also a demonstration of His strength to carry on, even though His closest friends had given in. Jesus resolved to finish what He started, even if others could not, and during a night above all nights, when He needed someone to stand with Him, He was left alone. Not only is the Father silent, but also now His friends are sleeping. When Jesus was pressed, the oil of strength flowed!

Later in this book, in chapter ten, I'll talk about the power of peers as we journey through the dark valley and how my life has been enriched and empowered by those who chose to stand with me. But even when we have good family and friends around us, there are still times when we will not only feel alone (and our feelings can play tricks on us), but we will be alone. When we are alone we're left with our own thoughts and feelings, and when no one is looking, no lights are shining on us and no friends are there to cheer us on, the decisions we make can define what the next day looks like.

It was 11.15pm and I was sitting in my hotel room having just taught for two hours at a church in London. I was tired and ready for bed, but that day the organisation I had served released a statement via Vimeo regarding my recent dismissal from a post I had held with them. No one had told me this was coming and I hadn't been consulted on the content. But as I hit the link, there it was, a statement about me to my world. As shock turned to sadness my room became *a painful press* as a range of emotions flooded through my body, finally resting on one of sadness.

A restless night followed my prayers and tears and the morning could not come quickly enough so I could just get home. However, in that hotel room I made two decisions. The first was that I would not respond, and the second that I would not give up! Though my heart was still heavy as I caught the train home, I knew I would survive this moment and it would soon be yesterday's news. But I also knew if I was going to thrive and not simply survive, I must not let this particular *press* crush my seed, however long it took for the oil to flow.

Don't look at your sleeping friends, look to the purpose for which you were called. During the times when they are not there to help you, go back to what you know, how, where and when you were called, the promises He made and the life you still have. Aloneness is a terribly difficult thing and though the enemy wants to use it to crush you, oil can flow from the decisions made in it that can not only change you, but your world. Don't walk away – walk on!

The Oil Of Steadfastness

The name Judas has become synonymous with betrayal, but it is the nature of his treachery that gives him a special place of infamy. Not only was Judas one of the inner circle of Jesus' friends (a group of twelve among many other disciples), but his signal of betrayal was a kiss! Jesus had washed his feet just a few hours before, perhaps in a final attempt of offering him an alternative route forward. But hardened by the offence he had *taken* from Jesus (Mark 14:1-11), Judas sold out his friend and sealed his own future. The depth of the betrayal is summed up in the words of Jesus Himself:

"He who shares My bread has lifted up his heel against Me." (John 13:18)

Jesus referenced Psalm 41:9 through which the depth of loss is even more apparent and therefore implied in His own words:

"Even my close friend, whom I trusted, he who shared my bread, has lifted up his heel against me."

Betrayal is one of the most difficult *presses* to endure, especially when it comes from those close to us. It is one thing to be "betrayed" by some stranger on social media, but quite another when it comes from someone you shared bread with. Such betrayal will provoke a response in us, and from my experience, it tends to be one of three that wins out.

#1 – Retreat

When the kiss of betrayal lands on our cheek, or lips, one of the most natural responses to such pain is to withdraw and back away from everything and anyone that might exacerbate the pain. Whatever the nature of the betrayal, the impulse to step back and step away is huge. However, Jesus did not retreat. If anything, He stepped forward to meet Judas. I would never seek to minimise betrayal nor the brokenness it causes, for I have experienced that once too often, but retreat ensures betrayal wins – not just at that moment, but also for as long as we disappear.

#2 – Retaliate

The act of betrayal in the garden is famous for the "ear cutting off" incident. As the guards stepped forward to arrest Jesus, some of His disciples stepped up to defend Him and John tells us that Simon Peter drew his sword and,

"...*struck the high priest's servant, cutting off his right ear. (The servant's name was Malchus)*." (John 18:10)

What is implied in the text is that Peter was probably not aiming for Malchus' ear (although if he was, Peter was a good swordsman), but rather he lashed out to inflict as much pain as possible on whoever was in his way.

When it comes to betrayal there's a Peter in us all. I'm not sure if I'm Jewish or Peter is Irish, or maybe we're both just human, but something inside me likes the idea of hitting back – although Judas would have been a better target than Malchus. If we're honest, however, we know that retaliation never works, because it doesn't give us back what we lost and in the process of cutting off someone's ear, we lose much more than we hoped to gain.

#3 - Rise

It's only Dr Luke who gives us the details of Jesus' response to this moment of hot headed madness from Peter:

"But Jesus answered, 'No more of this!' And He touched the man's ear and healed him." (Luke 22:51)

In the melee of the garden, where sleepy headed disciples were ready to rise up in armed conflict, Jesus stepped in and took control by rebuking the rebellion and healing Malchus' ear. But this action of Jesus was not simply an act of compassion to a young man who had lost his ear. Rather, this was a statement of intent, that even in the pressure of the press, Jesus was not going to allow anything to derail the reason He had come, or keep Him from drinking the Father's cup He had just agreed to drink. Jesus rose above the temptation to retreat and the instinct to retaliate by sticking to the purpose He had lived out for the previous three years. He had come to proclaim the year of God's favour, and this wasn't just for the multitudes of broken and lost sheep on the hillside, but this was for Malchus and everyone like him in the shrouded darkness of the olive press.

Someone kissed you and broke your heart, but don't retreat. If you do, you will disappear and the life God designed for you will disappear with you. I know you've been hurt, but don't retaliate. Leave your sword in its sheath. Lashing and slashing will feel good for a few mad moments, but when the fighting stops the cost will be greater than you ever dreamt of paying. Why not have the courage to rise above the brokenness and do something generous, kind and purpose-filled that will liberate you from the kiss of betrayal and the face of the betrayer? If you can find a way, then oil will flow, and where the betrayer was certain he had taken your seed, the Lord can bring forth a harvest of life.

The Oil Of Surrender

We get the impression that Jesus was taken from the garden, but John makes it clear He went! When the crowd of guards and soldiers approached with Judas, He went out to them and asked,

"'Who is it you want?' 'Jesus of Nazareth,' they replied. 'I am He,' Jesus said. When Jesus said, 'I am He,' they drew back and fell to the ground." (John 18:4-7)

This might have been the moment to charge, call the angels to come and show these unbelievers once and for all that Jesus really was "God in flesh". But instead, Jesus surrendered. John's Gospel was written that we might believe that Jesus is the Son of God[5], and carries seven glorious "I am" statements of Jesus – an unmistakable link to the phrase "I am that I am" that the Lord uses to describe Himself to Moses.[6] In John Jesus declares,

"I am the bread of life." (6:35)
"I am the light of the world." (8:12)
"I am the gate for the sheep." (10:7)
"I am the good shepherd." (10:11, 14)
"I am the resurrection and the life." (11:25)

"I am the way, the truth and the life." (14:6)
"I am the true vine." (15:1)

So when in the garden, Jesus declared "I am He", He was not simply letting everyone know that they had found Jesus of Nazareth, but that in fact, this "ordinary" man, was the incarnation of the Invisible God. Jesus was able to surrender to them because He knew who the Father was and trusted Him; that no matter what it looked like, His will would be done. He was able to surrender to them because He knew who He was, and no matter what it looked like, His identity would remain undiminished by their actions. When He surrendered to them it was not because He was weak, but because He was free!

Surrender can feel like failure and to an on-looking world that's what it might appear like, but surrender can also be one of our greatest acts of faith. When we say, "I surrender" because we know the Father and trust Him, the oil flows. When we say "I surrender" because we are secure in Him, even though it looks like *the press* has diminished us, the oil flows. When we say, "I surrender" because we believe there is a bigger and greater meaning to this moment, the oil flows.

I was once in a gathering of leaders with my father, when the leader asked me to describe my father in three words. Remember, he's sitting beside me. I knew my father would be deeply embarrassed by the attention, but in truth, this was an easy challenge as I summarised the character of the man I adored. The three words were, "Integrity, Honesty and Generosity". From August 2013 my father was pressed by the last great challenge of life, that of facing death, and yet as he was squeezed, over and over again oil came out. He maintained his love and worship of Jesus and even when he could no longer see to read his Bible, my mother would read it for him. He remained generous and kind to those around him and even in his own suffering he thought of others. The disease ravaging his lungs tried to take his seed, but served only in causing the oil within him to flow.

When I discovered what my father was suffering from, I was afraid for him. I had supported a member of my church whose father had died of the same thing and when the end came it wasn't pleasant for anyone. I prayed that if my father wasn't healed, that the Lord would make his passing as gentle as possible. On 9th December 2013, my gorgeous wee daddy passed into eternity. It all happened quickly and unexpectedly as he went from the living room of his home into heaven. As he closed his eyes, the last face he saw that day was the face of my mother, the woman he had loved so passionately and generously for almost sixty years of his life. But when he opened his eyes again, He saw the face of the Saviour, the One he had worshipped and served so faithfully from his first encounter as a ten-year-old, to his last breath, just seventy years later.

Gethsemane comes in many shapes and sizes, but always with the same intent, to search for oil. In the midst of the pressing, one phrase above all others will release the oil and save the seed: "Not as I will, but as You will."

When we drink the cup for Him, even what seems bitter can ultimately taste sweet.

Endnotes
1. Mt.26:36-56, Mk.14:32-52, Lk.22:39-53 & Jn.18:1-11. Luke and John don't reference the garden name specially, only Matthew and Mark do.
2. Aramaic - ga̱t šemānî = "oil press".
3. There is much debate about how olive oil was produced in ancient times and views on the impact on crushing the pit. For example see: http://www.academia.edu/29937641/Breaking_the_olive_pit_during_ancient_

and_modern_oil_making._Does_the_pit_affect_flavor_TRADE_AND_
PRODUCTION_IN_PREMONETARY_GREECE_Production_and_the_
Craftsman

4. The devil is not referenced in any of the four accounts, but in context of wider encounters, Gethsemane may be viewed as part of His ongoing spiritual conflict – see Lk.4:13

5. John 20:31

6. Exodus 3:14

Chapter Eight
Back Together Again – Word

"My comfort in my suffering is this:
Your promise preserves my life."
(Psalm 119:50)

For our 28th wedding anniversary, Dawn and I had the privilege of visiting Rome, a city we had always wanted to see and it did not disappoint. The weather was wonderful, the food incredible, it had coffee shops galore and, of course, gelato, lots of gelato! Of all the numerous and amazing sights to see in Rome, there was one monument on my list I did not want to miss out on, namely *The Arch of Titus*. You can find it on the Via Sacra just to the south west of the Roman Forum. Emperor Domitian built it in AD 82, after the death of his older brother Titus, to honour and commemorate his victories, which included the sacking of Jerusalem in AD 70.

On the south panel of the arch it records the spoils of war that were taken from the temple, including the gold trumpets, the fire pans for the ashes from the altar and the table of Shew Bread. But, even now, it is the Menorah that dominates the scene, the symbol of Judaism and the emblem on the coat of arms for modern Israel. However, the one item that is missing from the arch is the Word of God. Where everything else of significance was carried away, the Word is conspicuous by its absence.

Stripped of all the trappings of their religion, including land, temple and artefacts, Jews became known as the "People of the Book" (*Am HaSefer*), with it written on both their hearts and scrolls. It might be argued that a people survived because the Word lived within them! If there is one section of Scripture which shows this devotion and centrality of the Word of God, it is Psalm 119, the longest chapter in the Bible. God's Word is described in seven different ways, namely, law, statutes, precepts, decrees, commands, word and promise – and of the 176 verses within this psalm, only 6 do not mention the word in any shape or form[1] and the phrase "Your word(s)" occurs 27 times.[2] The psalm follows a simple, rhythmic pattern where each 8-verse section follows the letters of the Hebrew alphabet, giving 22 sections and 176 verses in total. The opening verse of this great psalm sets the tone for what is to come:

"Blessed are they whose ways are blameless, who walk according to the law of the Lord."

For those about to engage with the glories in this psalm, the first verse encourages them with the truth that if they walk according to God's Word and allow it to live within them and through them, then they will be blessed, because their lives will be complete, entire and sound.

Though the Gospels declare that Jesus is the Word, they also make it clear that He loved the Word. The Hebrew Bible (what Christians refer to as the Old Testament) was the only Bible Jesus had, and He used it well. Divided into three sections we have the *Torah* (instruction), the *Nevi'im* (the Prophets) and *Ketuvim* (the writings) – in totality referred to as *Tanakh*. From my research of the Gospels, Jesus quoted from every book of the five in the Torah (the engine room of the Old Testament), with Deuteronomy being His favourite. Of the Prophets He quoted Isaiah the most, and when it comes to the Writings, the only book He referenced was Psalms. As recorded by the Gospels, I estimate that Jesus quoted (directly or indirectly) the Scriptures on at least 104 separate occasions, only one of which He read from a scroll, while all the rest were from memory.[3] Jesus loved the Word!

Without the Word of God in my life, I am certain I would not have survived the valley I had to walk through. As the psalmist puts it,

"If Your law had not been my delight, I would have perished in my affliction." (Psalm 119:92)

If we are to journey through the dark valleys of life and find restoration in our brokenness, then there is no substitute for the Word of God. Whatever or whoever else supports us, the Word of God is the one thing that is going to help "put us back together again". Without the Word we're left with positive psychology and Twitter philosophy – which can provide us with an inspirational shot in the arm, but cannot truly renew our minds and transform our lives. In order to survive the valley and find power in the pain, we must engage with the Word that comes from the mouth of God. His Word alone can save us, heal us, restore us and empower us to move forward with purpose. As we are reminded in the psalm:

"The law from Your mouth is more precious to me than thousands of pieces of silver and gold." (Psalm 119:72)

I had the privilege of being raised in a home where the Word of God was honoured and the opportunity to grow up in a spiritual context where reading, memorising and studying the Word was encouraged. I have a stack of old Bibles that have walked with me since my teenage years, and I have studied seriously the Bible all my adult life. In these last few years, the power of His Word has manifest itself in the darkest valley in such a way that it has literally sustained me through the journey. When the lights have gone out, friends have gone home and the atmosphere has vanished, it has been the relentless power of His Word that has kept me.

So what has the Word done for me as I've walked through the pain?

His Word Has Challenged My Focus

"Your word, O Lord, is eternal; it stands firm in the heavens. Your faithfulness continues through all generations; You established the earth, and it endures." (Psalm 119:89-90)

I have been reminded again that the Word I hold in my hand and heart, is not just any word, it is His Word. His Word is a representation of His character and purpose, so what I've received is not just human wisdom with a spiritual jacket but God's wisdom. The Word I have is "God-breathed", containing the very life of God, thus reminding me that when I read the words His breath can bring life to me through those words, because His life is within them. When the Word of God comes (in whatever form), its primary role is to point the recipient to the Word-Giver Himself – thus challenging our focus with a view to transforming our thinking. If we are honest, we tend to focus on the "what is God going to do for me" bit of the Word, when really He wants to lift our eyes beyond that to see the One who gave the Word in the first place. In my valley, the Word has challenged my focus by moving it from what He will do for me (which is still important) to Who He is.

As part of my devotional cycle over the last two years, I have deliberately spent time meditating on the 26 names or titles of God, rotating my reflections twice per year thus covering 52 weeks. As I've turned to one of His names each day, it has been a transformative experience. It has forced me to take the focus off myself and shift focus onto Him, deepening my appreciation for and worship of Him. This has been good for me. As we've seen already, pain and brokenness tend to draw our focus onto ourselves, and over a prolonged period of suffering this has the ability to reduce our world to powerless introversion. Pain-induced self-centredness has a tendency to inflate our needs and deflate God to the One who can meet those needs. Thus, slowly and subtly, our devotions become more about *us* than about *Him*.

David put it beautifully when he said,

"How lovely is Your dwelling place, O Lord Almighty! My soul yearns, even faints, for the courts of the Lord; My heart and flesh cry out for the Living God." (Psalm 84:1-2)

At times, my pain transformed my want for Him into wanting Him "for me", thus reducing Him to my needs and the challenges I faced, when He wanted to lift me up to see His greatness in the midst of it all. Confronted by the Word, I've had to come to a place of repentance for the presence of this subtle idolatry in my life. I am learning that if I come to His Word looking for Him, I often find the answers I need.

His Word Has Created Faith

"Open my eyes that I may see wonderful things in Your law." (Psalm 119:18)

Each morning when I pick up the Bible, I kiss it and recite this verse because I know I need to see things beyond my own intellect and reason in order to truly engage with the supernatural Lord I serve. I know that if I approach His Word naturally, then I'll see it only with my natural eyes, but if I am open to the supernatural dimension of His truth, then I might receive something that can change my mind and my life. These moments of revelation, when our eyes are opened, are crucial because this is where faith is created within us. Paul helps us with this when he concludes,

"...faith comes from hearing the message, and the message is heard through the word of Christ." (Romans 10:17)

When the Lord speaks and we truly hear or see, it is a moment of faith, out of which mountains can move and valleys can be traversed. Hearing His Word brings us to a place of knowing which allows us to say "I know" when everyone around us is asking, "Are you sure?" This confession is not an attempt to twist God's arm up His back with our agenda wrapped in Bible verses, rather this is our mouth agreeing with our heart agreeing with the Word we have seen and heard from the Lord. It is from this faith, created by His Word, that we find the strength to go on and the power to overcome.

On the week it was being announced that I was being removed from my post as Principal of Mattersey Hall, the Assemblies of God Bible college, I reached one of my lowest emotional points. Not only were we two weeks away from Simeon's trial, but the world, my world, was about to hear I no longer had a job. The announcement was going live on the Wednesday of that week, but as I woke on Monday morning, I felt horrible. I lacked energy and had my emotions been allowed to drive the agenda, I would have been on the next transport to Mars. But I got up, made my first cup of coffee and sat in silence in the presence of God.

I didn't want to read or pray I just wanted to sit. But as I looked at the Book, something within me stirred and I picked it up. I kissed it, prayed and opened it. As part of my readings I was in Isaiah and that week would cover Isaiah chapters 41-47. But as I read Isaiah 41 the Lord spoke so powerfully that faith arose within me. Though the morning had started so miserably it had been transformed in minutes by a word from God; a word that sustained me through the next few horrible days. Had I not picked up the Book that day, I may have missed His word and the faith that it created in me. The experience of that morning taught me again (as if I didn't already know), to pick up the Book, read the Book and listen to the Book, even when it is the last thing I feel like doing.

We can't *faith* faith, because faith comes from His Word. That's why the enemy will do all he can to separate you from it because he knows first hand its power. Pick it up, open it, read it and dare to believe that your eyes may be opened to see and understand wonderful things in His law.

His Word Has Instilled Fortitude

"My soul faints with longing for Your salvation, but I have put my hope in Your word." (Psalm 119:81)

This theme of putting hope in His Word runs throughout this psalm, repeated on at least three other occasions, namely verses 74 (witness), 114 (protection) and 147 (help). In each case the idea for hope is the same, that of looking forward to something and waiting for the arrival of some resolution or deliverance. Even if nothing immediate happens, the writer will remain fixed on the word given to him by the Lord. There is a direct connection between the Word and the strength needed to walk through the valley, and the psalmist has placed his hope in the Word as the means to sustain and strengthen him. This is captured succinctly for us when he concludes,

"Though I am like a wineskin in the smoke, I do not forget Your decrees." (v83)

"They almost wiped me from the earth, but I have not forsaken Your precepts." (v87)

In both cases, the situation is tough and difficult and it seems unresolved, but he makes a decision to "not forget" and "not forsake" the Word of the Lord, for he knows if he does so, all will be lost.

The definition of fortitude is to have "courage in pain or adversity" and has come to the English language from a Latin word (via French), *fortis*, which means "strong", from which we also get the word fortress. Fortitude is the strength to keep going *in* the pain, *in* the adversity and *in* the valley. This is not a courage that comes from our personality type or the fear of failure, this is courage that comes from the truth that we dare to believe, no matter what circumstances confront us. So often we try to work courage up and I've found that just doesn't help, at least not in the long term, for such courage relies on me. This is fine as long as I am okay and I have enough fuel in my tank or the strength of personality to keep me going. When His Word is the source of our strength, however, then we're not looking in on ourselves, we're looking up to Him and we find something much greater than anything we could have found within.

Putting our hope in His Word is a challenge, because it is the admission that we cannot do it in our own strength or ability, but need the Lord to help us. But the payoff for such humility can be staggering, as this opens the door for the Lord to work in us and demonstrate His power and glory in ways that did not seem possible. Isaiah puts it magnificently:

"The Lord is the everlasting God, the Creator of the ends of the

earth. He will not grow tired or weary, and His understanding no one can fathom. He gives strength to the weary and increases the power of the weak. Even youths grow tired and weary, and young men stumble and fall; but those who hope in the Lord will renew their strength. They will soar on wings like eagles; they will run and not grow weary, they will walk and not faint." (Isaiah 40:28-31)

Weariness is a theme that runs through this passage, mentioned in one form or another four times, but the answer to our weariness, being worn out by the toil of life, is finding a place of "hope in the Lord". When the Word of God touches our soul it produces courage and strength that empowers us to walk, run and fly. That's why we need it and that's why the enemy will do everything in his power to keep us from it, for he knows when the Word lives in us, we are truly alive!

His Word Has Produced Fruit

"Your promises have been thoroughly tested, and Your servant loves them." (Psalm 119:140)

When we think of the fruit that comes from the promises of God, we usually mean the fulfilment of the promise and any positive outcomes associated with it.

- The Lord promised a child and the child was born
- The Lord promised me a better job and I got it
- The Lord promised me a car and here it is

But if the valley has taught me anything about God's Word it is that it yields fruit not only at fulfilment, but in the process towards fulfilment, and these are the lessons we normally miss because we're in such a rush to get the baby, the promotion or the car! Some of the things the Lord has promised me still haven't been fulfilled, but His Word is bearing fruit nonetheless as I move towards the outworking of His promise. However, because we're so focused on what the Lord will do for us, often what He does for us in the meantime can feel like the "second prize". Yet, what we learn on the way can be as life-transforming as that which we get at the end.

Psalms 19 highlights this principle so clearly for us:

"The law of the Lord *is* perfect, *reviving the soul.*
The statutes of the Lord *are* trustworthy, *making wise the simple.*
The precepts of the Lord *are* right, *giving joy to the heart.*
The commands of the Lord *are* radiant, *giving light to the eyes.*
The fear of the Lord *is* pure, enduring for ever.
The ordinances of the Lord are sure and altogether righteous.
They are more precious than gold, than much pure gold;
They are sweeter than honey, than honey from the comb.
By them Your servant *is* warned; in keeping them *there is great reward.*" (v7-11)

I've highlighted certain phrases and words in italics because I wanted to show the immediacy of the power of His Word to us, as well as the long term pay off. When we are in the valley, the only thing we want to do is get out of it, and why not, so we tend to cling onto the words that offer that hope. But these verses show us that we can find rich, if unexpected fruit, as we journey through the valley; fruit that we can enjoy now, not just when we find the exit.

When it comes to the Word of the Lord, don't just look

forward to what will be, but look around to what is now. See what His Word is producing and giving you right now and you might be surprised by what you find. In the journey I've been on, there have been many days when I just wanted to get out of the valley and have the sun on my face, celebrating the goodness of the Lord. But I have learned that even in the trial, the pain and the brokenness, His Word has been at work in me and that at a time of my own struggle, His Word has produced glorious fruit.

Extravagant – When Worship Becomes Lifestyle[4], my previous book, was written entirely in the dark valley. It was released in September 2016 in between being informed of my dismissal from my ministry post and the trial of my son. Though I had wanted to write this book for years and finally believed it was time to do so, it was in many ways the worst time to write it. There were days when I didn't want to write and when I didn't feel like writing, and there were moments when I felt that what I had written was rubbish. Yet, the book and the teaching that has come from it has blessed so many people, even becoming a seven-day devotional on the @YouVersion Bible app, where thousands have completed it. Every time I look at that book, I'm reminded that His Word produces fruit, even in the valley of brokenness.

Paul tells us:

"All Scripture is God-breathed and is useful for teaching, rebuking, correcting and training in righteousness, so that the man of God may be thoroughly equipped for every good work." (2 Timothy 3:16-17)

Because this verse is located in a letter written by a leader to a leader, many tend to interpret this in terms of ministry and service, but to do so is to miss out on the power at the heart of this text. Whoever you are and wherever you are, His Word to you is God-breathed and can be to you everything you need for the moment you are in. There is life within His Word, life that can sustain you in the valley and empower you out of the valley. But, we have an enemy who knows the power of God's Word, and who to our first parents asked the question, "Did God really say?"[5] and to Jesus Himself asked, "*If* You are the Son of God?"[6] He will audaciously challenge the Word of God within us, because he knows if he can separate us from the Word then we are noise without substance and heat without power. He doesn't mind what you do, as long as you do it without the Word.

So I encourage you,

Read the Word

Make time every day to read it. I have been a Christian since I was eight years old and I still have a Bible reading plan. The Bible is the greatest book you own and there is nothing in your library that compares to its magnificence. Don't allow it to gather dust, but make it a daily companion on your pilgrimage. Somebody once said, "When we pray we talk to God, but when we read the Word, God talks to us." Give the Lord a chance to talk to you today by opening the Book.

Chew the Word

Don't just read it, but learn to chew on it. Reading the Bible is not a race nor a competition, it's the means of getting divine truth into your soul, so slow down and give it a chance to digest and live. I would rather you read one chapter per day but chewed on it, reflected on it and got lots of goodness out of it, than read six chapters a day then forget what you'd read. What's the point in that?

Confess the Word

If the Lord has spoken to you and His Word has become revelation to you, then speak it out. That doesn't necessarily mean putting it on Twitter for the whole world to see, but at least start in your own room and perhaps in the safety of your own world, and speak out what you've seen and what you've heard. Let the revealed Word become the confessed Word, for there is power in revelation confession. Don't wait until you're out of the valley, do it now when there's no sign of the exit.

Live the Word

When the Lord speaks, do what He says. In our dark valley, we have done things that did not make sense at the time, but which we believed the Lord told us to do. Obedience is possible even in brokenness and pain, and to do the right thing even when we don't feel great about it. Obedience to the Word is the greatest sign that we believe, even though we can't see how it's all going to work out. Obedience gets the Lord's attention in the valley of darkness.

Over 2000 years ago, Romans destroyed Jerusalem and the temple, enslaving and dispersing its people and carrying away their most precious religious symbols. To any onlooker of that day it seemed like the end for the Jews as they entered the darkest valley of all. Yet, today, a nation has been reborn and Jerusalem has been rebuilt, while *The Arch of Titus* sits in the midst of the crumbling ruins of the once great Roman Empire. The Romans took everything but the one thing that really counted … The Word!

The enemy may attempt to take all we hold dear, but what He really wants is the Word. If we hold on to it then the Word will hold us up. As long as we have it within us, then no valley can hold us, no pain can cripple us, and brokenness cannot destroy us. Our enemy knows the Book and all it contains can put us back together again.

"May the words of my mouth and the meditation of my heart be pleasing in Your sight, O Lord, my Rock, and my Redeemer."
(Psalm 19:14)

Endnotes
1. Verses 3, 84, 90, 121, 122 and 132 – 6 in Hebrew points to the number of man
2. (Words of You in Hebrew) - verses 9, 11, 16, 17, 25, 28, 37, 42, 49, 57, 65, 67, 74, 81, 89, 101, 103, 105, 107, 114, 130, 133, 139, 147, 158, 169 & 172
3. In Luke 4 Jesus reads from the scroll of the Prophet Isaiah
4. *Extravagant* was published in 2016 by River Publishing and is also available on Kindle
5. Genesis 3:1
6. Luke 4:3

Chapter Nine
Back Together Again – Worship
[The Power of Presence]

"Seven times a day I praise You for Your righteous laws."
(Psalm 119:164)

The two men sat shivering in the darkness, no doubt a combination of the cold and shock. They had been stripped, beaten and then severely flogged. Now they lay on a prison floor, their feet in stocks and their prospects bleak. But somewhere in the darkness, in the valley in which they now found themselves, they began to pray and sing praises to God. In their moment of brokenness, worship rose from their hearts, through their lips and into the horror of the prison, ensuring that their "disappointed" would not become disappointment. Though their bodies were bruised, their backs were scarred and their ankles were bleeding, they found a way to move beyond broken and in the most unlikely of places. They discovered power in the pain![1]

Growing up in church I remember singing a song:
It's amazing what praising can do, hallelujah, hallelujah.
It's amazing what praising can do, hallelujah.

I don't worry when things go wrong,
Jesus fills my heart with song.
It's amazing what praising can do, hallelujah.[2]

Songs like this seem quaint and out dated today, but the heart of its message is profound and correct. When we learn to praise God, whatever circumstances we find ourselves in, something amazing can take place. Dr Luke tells us,

"About midnight Paul and Silas were praying and singing hymns to God..." (Acts 16:25)

They had no lights, band or atmosphere to help them, but in the absence of all the aids to worship so many of us enjoy today, they dug deep into the Word within them and created their own worship concert, transforming the context they were in. Had both men remained silent, no one would have blamed them and everyone would have understood. After all, they had endured a horrendous experience. But they refused to be silent. Instead, their praise transformed a dungeon into a throne, inviting the Lord to sit among them.

Learning to praise in the *prison* is one of the keys to finding power in the pain. When we find ourselves in places we neither want to be, nor deserve to be, our confessional response is crucial. It can determine whether we remain trapped as victims of injustice, or rise to the victory of freedom (even if the chains remain attached).

As I've walked through the dark valley, I've had to learn the *practice of praise* and it has been this story in particular that has encouraged me when praise was the last thing I felt like doing. Sometimes the practice of praise has been in public, surrounded by brothers and sisters in Christ – and what a blessing it is to worship in community. Sometimes it has been with just a few close friends, as together we've raised our hearts toward heaven. However, many times, dare I say, most times, I have learned to break through in the practice of praise on my own, when it has just been me, the Word and the Lord. With no one to hear my song, I nonetheless learned to sing. With no words on the screen, I learned to speak out the Word of truth. In rooms without atmosphere I discovered the power of His presence. The dungeon in Philippi remains the greatest worship seminar I have ever attended. The lessons learned, I share with you.

The Practice of Praise Places God Over Self

"... *Paul and Silas were praying and singing hymns to God...*" (Acts 16:25)

We can't be certain of the content of their prayers, nor of the hymns they sang, but we do know that they were towards God. Silas was not looking to Paul, nor Paul to Silas, for an exit strategy. Instead they were looking upwards to the Lord, and by that very action, were taking their eyes off themselves. At a time when the temptation to look inward was probably at its peak, Paul and Silas made a decision to *look up* and worship the Lord. It is fascinating that when Paul later writes to the church at Philippi, planted out of this very visit, he remarks,

"*Rejoice in the Lord always. I will say it again: Rejoice!*" (Philippians 4:4)

Paul had some authority to make such a statement, not simply because it was true, but because he had personally demonstrated its power when in Philippi. He understood that if we learn to take our eyes off of self, and place them on the Lord, anything can happen and most likely will.

It was while reading Psalm 119 that I came across verse 164:

"*Seven times a day I praise You for Your righteous laws.*"

In response to that word, I decided to praise Him. It would have been easy to fixate on the opening verse of the section, which reads,

"Rulers persecute me without cause..." (v161)

But instead I worshipped. For the next forty-five minutes or so that morning, I remembered every good thing the Lord had given me or done for me and rehearsed them openly before Him. In those moments I forgot about my pain and the injustice I felt, and I lifted my eyes to Him, giving Him praise. Though nothing changed in my circumstances that day, something changed in me!

Praise reminds us how good the Lord is, regardless of our circumstances. It challenges our position of centrality in the season of pain. Praise dethrones self and enthrones the Lord – that's what makes it so powerful. At its heart, we are coming back to *who He is* and, by implication, what He can do or has done.

The Practice of Praise Places Confession Over Condition

The condition of these men is graphically spelled out for us by Dr Luke:

"... dragged into the market place..." (Acts 16:19)
"... stripped and beaten..." (v22)
"... severely flogged..." (v23)
"... thrown into prison..." (v23)
"... he put them in the inner cell..." (v24)
"... fastened their feet in stocks..." (v24)

Even a quick glance of these words gives us an insight into their condition. Of course, it wasn't the first or last time Paul and his companions would experience such things, as persecution seemed to be an expected norm for 1st Century believers. However, it is too easy to skim over their suffering and fail to empathise with the reality of their predicament. And the fact is, the songs they sang came at a time when their bruises were still fresh! Paul and Silas decided to lift the Lord over their condition, even though it remained unchanged. Imagine the potential criticism that might come their way when declaring, "The Lord is good and His love endures forever." The only sound accompanying their singing was the noise of their chains rattling!

I love football and as a Liverpool supporter I have grown up with the expectation that the crowd, sometimes referred to as the "twelfth man", will cheer the team on, no matter what the score. The last thing any team wants to hear from their supporters is silence or booing. In fact, one of the tactics of any good team is to try and silence the other team's supporters by playing so well. I have seen managers and players waving frantically to the crowd in an attempt to get them to sing more or turn up the volume. If you ever go to a football match, you might hear a taunting chant to the fans of the losing side, "You only sing when you're winning. Sing when you're winning, you only sing when you're winning!" The words may be simple, but their message is devastatingly profound.

Pain and brokenness is one of the ways the enemy attempts to "silence the crowd" and gets us to turn down our praise. As one whose job it was to lead praises to the Lord in Heaven, Satan knows the power of praise and craves for himself what should only ever go to God. So if he cannot have our praise, then he will do all he can to ensure that the Lord doesn't get it. Imagine what might happen if we learned to sing when it seems like we're not winning. The idea sounds crazy, and might look a bit odd to some, but it declares that the condition we find ourselves in shall not win. Instead we will lift up the Lord over our condition or circumstances. Even with scars we sing, and in spite of the bruises we bless; when it looks like we are powerless, we praise!

It is not always easy to maintain our confession when the circumstances we're facing seem to contradict what we're saying. But this comes back to our confidence in the word the Lord has given to us. His word will not return to Him without accomplishing what He sent it to do – even when, from our perspective, there are moments when His word doesn't seem to be doing very much.

Paul had entered the region of Macedonia as a result of a direct word from the Lord, through a vision. Having twice been prevented from going where he wanted to, it was at Troas that Paul received the "Macedonian call" and promptly obeyed.[3] So he wasn't in Philippi for a holiday, or even because he thought it might be a good place to go – he was there because he heard God tell him to go. Yet, even with the memory of the call fresh in his mind, he found himself in prison, on the wrong end of injustice. But even though he was confronted with this apparent contradiction of faith, he made a decision to lift up his praise and confession to the Lord. He may not have expected to be in prison, but he knew he was still in the palm of the Lord's hand.

Whatever the Lord has said, keep confessing it over your life and your world, regardless of the circumstances that confront you. The bruises, scars and chains will try to mock you; to taunt you to shut up; but that is the very moment to sing – to sing loud and sing clear. Such songs always rise to the top of heaven's charts!

The Practice of Praise Places Faith Over Feelings

"About midnight…" (Acts 16:25)

I love the seemingly incidental details of the text, yet everything Dr Luke records speaks of the power of this experience. He tells us that the turning point of the ordeal was around midnight – the moment at which one day disappears and a new day begins. A moment when Paul and his friend would normally be in bed, resting. It's a halfway point, with darkness having fallen at around 6.00pm the previous evening, and the dawn of a rising sun still 5-6 hours away. Midnight was a liminal place for Paul and Silas, where the darkness was at its greatest, time at its slowest, and perhaps their pain at its most intense. Yet, at the most vulnerable hour, they made a decision to praise the Lord and not allow their feelings to drive their declaration.

There is something about the darkness and stillness of the night that exaggerates our loneliness and exasperates our pain. If ever our feelings play tricks on us, it's then. I've discovered it's in the darkest hours of the night that every issue has the potential to grow in size.

In August 2016 we were enjoying a wonderful holiday in Zimbabwe, and as part of that trip, Dawn and I visited Victoria Falls (another bucket list item for any traveller). Friends Alan and Dorothy Graham had unexpectedly and generously blessed us with a wonderful hotel, and in the midst of our turmoil we found an oasis of peace. However, on the first night at the Falls, I was woken around 2.00am (I normally sleep well), by the presence of something in the room. It was so strong that I was convinced someone was in the room with us. I sat up in bed trying not to wake Dawn, and as my eyes adjusted to the gloom I realised to my relief that no one was there. However, the feeling of evil didn't leave and it started to intimidate my soul. My thoughts turned to my son and his trial and the fact that I was out of a job, even though at that stage it had not been announced. Fear and doubt began to grip my soul. But as they did so, I began to speak out in a whisper the name of Jesus and my love for Him. The more I spoke, the more the power of the Spirit rose within me and I became stronger in my worship and more determined in my faith. I lay back down and continued bringing to mind the promises of God, speaking out the names of the Lord and declaring my faith that whatever happened, "I would see the goodness of the Lord in the land of the living." This lasted for around twenty-five minutes and then suddenly, the evil presence I had felt vanished. At that exact moment, the Lord spoke to me from the Scriptures and gave me a promise that has sustained me from that day until this.

Feelings are normal and natural, but they should not, and cannot, be trusted when it comes to issues of faith. If we allow those midnight feelings to direct our thoughts, we'll quickly surrender to the hopelessness of fear and the impotence of doubt. Faith is one of the keys to combating the onslaught of our midnight feelings, for faith brings us back to what we know and leads us away from how we feel. As the writer to the Hebrews declares:

"Now faith is being sure of what we hope for and certain of what we do not see." (Hebrews 11:1)

The power of faith is that it does not need, nor relies upon, our feelings to operate. Rather, as we've seen, it finds its origin in God's Word. Because of this, faith can face down and take control of our feelings, and one of the vehicles that allows this to happen is praise. As we sing and confess, even at midnight, we give faith the chance to fight the terror of the darkness and bring to us the light of His life.

The Practice of Praise Places Witness Over Woes

"... and the other prisoners were listening to them." (Acts 16:25)

Imagine if Paul and Silas had sat on the floor and complained about the Lord and the predicament they were in? What impact would words of discouragement, disappointment and disillusionment have had on the unseen witnesses of their conversation? Whether Paul and Silas knew it or not, prisoners were listening to both their prayers and their songs. Nowhere in the text does it say that any of them asked for prayer or joined in with the songs, but they were listening, and the chances are, they were hearing something they had never heard before. In a prison, one expects to hear expressions of selfishness, anger, regret and even confusion. But when the noise coming from the most secure and uncomfortable cell in the building was that of prayers and hymns to God, people took notice and paid attention. Their *practice of praise* became a vehicle for witness, opening a door of opportunity that would have been lost, had they succumbed to the natural temptation of telling a tale of woe.

Our world has come to expect words of negativity from our experience of pain and brokenness. At such moments, it is generally ready to join in with us, affirming us in our misery. But when praise and worship flows out of us, it has the power to stop people in their tracks. How they react is not our responsibility, for some will react cynically, thinking we're crazy or deceived, while others will reflect on what they've heard and dare to question where such praise comes from. Living a life of praise and speaking words of worship in the midst of our own pain can be one of the greatest witnesses to our family, friends and wider world, speaking of the strength of our faith and perhaps even the goodness of our God. Whether we believe it

143

or not, people are listening to and watching us. I'm sure we've all had the experience of someone picking us up on stuff we did wrong or things we said that were inappropriate. So if they spot the negative, doesn't it follow they'll also be impacted by the positive – whether they acknowledge it or not? Paul and Silas didn't speak to the prisoners but to the Lord, but what they said to the Lord, spoke to the prisoners!

Your praise speaks and it will have more of an impact than you know. When our world sees us suffer just like them, but our reactions are different from theirs, maybe, just maybe, our witness will give them hope in their prison. As a follower of Jesus I believe in the blessing that comes from "fearing and following the Lord" and I have seen my life lift physically, socially, educationally and financially. I take great delight in telling people that all I am and have is because of His grace. But as a follower of Jesus I've also experienced pain, loss, sickness, sorrow, death and unemployment, and in those challenges I must also find a voice that declares my faith in the Lord who is *still* good, *still* kind, *still* generous and *still* in control. The praise that arises from our prosperity speaks to our world, but could it be that the praise that arises from our adversity speaks a little louder?

Look at the outcome of Paul and Silas' *practice of praise*:

"Suddenly there was such a violent earthquake that the foundations of the prison were shaken. At once all the prison doors flew open, and everybody's chains came loose." (Acts 16:26)

As they prayed and praised, three dynamic things occurred.

Firstly, the supernatural flooded into the natural

As chains fell off and prison doors flew open, the supernatural power of the Lord entered the hopeless darkness of the prison. God's power was made manifest in an impossible situation and through an improbable event, and the Lord used Paul and Silas' praise to work His purpose in the situation.

Our *practice of praise* can open a door for the Lord to open doors for us. As we break through our barriers of self, context, feelings and woes, the Lord can break into any situation on our behalf and manifest His glory. His "suddenly" can come at a time when we least expect it, because in part, we have not let go of Him or our confession in the midnight hour.

Secondly, others benefited from their blessing

As a result of that event, the jailer asked the question,

"'Sirs, what must I do to be saved?' They replied, 'Believe in the Lord Jesus, and you will be saved – you and your household.' Then they spoke the word of the Lord to him and to all the others in his house." (Acts 16:30-32)

At that moment we realise that the earthquake and the supernatural intervention of the Lord wasn't for Paul and Silas, but for the nameless jailer and his household. The Lord could have sent an angel to get Paul and Silas out of prison, as He had done for Peter before.[4] But this action wasn't for them, rather it was for a house full of people who were lost. As Paul and Silas lifted their eyes up to heaven, the Lord demonstrated that His plan was much bigger than ministering to their pain. It seems their praise took them much further than the boundaries their pain would ever have allowed.

Our *practice of praise* can be the voice the Lord needs to speak into someone else's darkness. The jailer got to hear the Lord because Paul and Silas refused to be silent. His Word can come to others because of our witness in chains and sometimes, others can find His salvation because we maintained our confession in our suffering.

Thirdly, they experienced freedom before release

"When it was daylight, the magistrates sent their officers to the jailer with the order, 'Release those men.'" (Acts 16:35)

All of this happened around midnight, but Paul and Silas weren't released until daylight. But what is clear is that both men were free long before the prison door opened. In their own imprisonment they ministered to others, and in serving brought the glory of the kingdom. It is a striking idea, that the jailer, after food and celebration, would have returned Paul and Silas back to their cell, pending the decision of the magistrate. Even though the Lord did a miracle and the jailer got saved, Paul and Silas were still incarcerated. Yet they clearly found freedom before release.

Our *practice of praise* can set us free even if our context does not change. The paradox of such an event teaches us that the Lord can do something in us, for and through us, while the chains remain in place. It is natural to want the prison door to open and permit our escape. But sometimes the door remains closed – not because the Lord doesn't want to rescue us from our suffering, but so that we can find freedom in it.

As I reflect with you on the practice of praise, permit me to say one more thing that isn't in the text we've considered – namely the practice of speaking in Tongues. Regarded as one of the nine gifts of the Spirit,[5] Paul says,

"He who speaks in a tongue edifies himself ... For if I pray in a tongue, my spirit prays, but my mind is fruitful ... I thank God that I speak in tongues more than all of you." (1 Corinthians 14:4, 14, 18)

The gift of tongues is a grace gift given by the Holy Spirit to help followers of Jesus grow and go in His name. From Paul's teaching to the church at Corinth, there seems to be two uses of it. The first is public – that is, to the gathered community of believers. But in this context Paul says if this is going to happen, then someone needs to be present who has the gift of Interpretation, so everyone can understand. The second is private – that is, I'm not speaking in tongues for the benefit of others, but for myself. My spirit is speaking to God's Spirit and, as I do so, somehow, supernaturally I am being built up and strengthened in my spirit. Though in public, Paul encouraged the gift of Prophecy, because everyone could understand that, he also confessed that he spoke in tongues more than anyone, clearly pointing to this more private practice.

From this teaching I believe that speaking in tongues is like a high-speed broadband connection to God. Though my mind doesn't know what's being spoken, my spirit is uploading to the Spirit of God and He is downloading to me. The devil can't break this connection and, as I speak mysteries, I am being supernaturally built up. In my valley I have found this practice to be invaluable, for when my mind runs out of words, or when in extreme moments my pain stunts my words, speaking in tongues has taken me beyond the limitation of my intellect into a supernatural confession that is working miraculously on my behalf. If you can speak in tongues, I encourage you to make it part of your *practice of praise.*

Paul and Silas found themselves in the dark valley of prison, but in their suffering they raised a voice of praise that enabled them to find freedom before their release. In a context that screamed "be quiet", they prayed and sang hymns to God. Through that simple act of defiant praise, they rose up out of

147

their despair and invited the Lord into their cell.

Whatever our prison looks like, the *practice of praise* can transform us in it, even if we're not delivered from it.

> *"From the rising of the sun to the place where it sets,*
> *the name of the Lord is to be praised."*
> (Psalm 113:3)

Endnotes
1. Read the story in full Acts 16:11-40
2. By Al Matthews and Rebecca Mullens
3. Acts 16:6-10
4. Acts 12:1-19
5. 1 Corinthians 12:1-11

Chapter Ten
Back Together Again – Walk

[The Power of Peers]

"A friend loves at all times, and a brother is born for adversity."
(Proverbs 17:17)

True friendship is invaluable when traversing the valley of brokenness and when trying to find power in the pain. As we've observed already, Elijah deliberately left his servant behind because he thought that dying in the wilderness would be much easier if no one was around. I have been blessed with a wonderful community of people around me all of my life. I was born into a loving and generous family and today I am secure in the love of my own family. I've always had good friends at every stage of my journey and been enriched in so many ways by the input of outstanding people. Truly, the people around me have made me look much better than I am. I've known and appreciated this truth for a long time.

Yet, in these last few years, I have come to appreciate even more deeply an understanding of friendship forged in the crucible of adversity and honed in the dark valley. It might be an exaggeration to say that without these friends, I may have been lost, because in the valley the Lord has been with me, and He has been my Helper. However, it is true to say that without them, the journey would have been less joyous and more arduous. Although, with the Lord's strength, I have emerged through the challenges, I am eternally grateful for those who never let me walk alone.

People sometimes get the impression that Paul, often referred to as the Apostle Paul, was a lone-ranger type character, who because of his unique brilliance was self-sufficient; able to blast a path alone for Jesus across the first century world. But nothing could be further from the truth. When we study Paul carefully, we find a uniquely brilliant man with high levels of energy and relentless zeal to reach the world for Jesus, but we also see a man investing in people, building team and walking with friends.

Throughout his letters, Paul refers over and over to those who are working with him. In Romans chapter 16, he lists 37 individuals, named or referenced, 10 of whom are women. Writing to the church in Philippi, one of Paul's most personal letters, we get a further glimpse of this relational reality as he highlights in particular the input of two young men, namely Timothy and Epaphroditus. When speaking of Timothy, he not only holds him up as a son, but as an outstanding, selfless servant. Paul says,

"I have no one else like him, who takes a genuine interest in your welfare" and goes on to say, *"But you know that Timothy has proved himself, because as a son with his father he has served with me in the work of the gospel"* (Philippians 2:20, 22).

Even though Timothy was a *son*, he wasn't working *for* Paul, rather he was working *with him*.

As if to further emphasise his relational heart, Paul then

highlights Epaphroditus, describing him in three dynamic ways: *"...my brother, fellow-worker and fellow-soldier..."* (Philippians 2:25)

We can observe the layers of the relationship between the two men, moving from brother, *someone with me*, to fellow-worker, *someone working with me*, to fellow-soldier, *someone who fights with and for me*. Epaphroditus encapsulates such a range of commitment to Paul, that Paul has to use three different words to describe this young man. It's as we break these words down even further that we see the depth of Paul's appreciation and the strength of their friendship.

Brother: the word Paul uses here is *adelphós* and it points to the idea of coming from the same womb. By calling Epaphroditus brother this is not just a reference to him being in Christ with Paul, but the fact that the two men have a heart bond, as if born from the same mother. A common faith in Jesus may have brought them together, but something more is keeping them together.

Fellow-worker: the word Paul uses here is *sunergós* from *sún*, "together with", and *érgon*, "work". What a beautiful thought at the heart of this word, that Paul saw Epaphroditus as someone working *together with* him, rather than merely working for him. Epaphroditus wasn't simply serving Paul, sent as a messenger of the church at Philippi, but Paul saw him as a "side by side" worker. In fact, this is one of Paul's favourite words when describing those on his team. It occurs 13 times in the New Testament and Paul uses it 12 of those 13 times.[1]

Fellow-soldier: the word Paul uses here is *sustratiôtēs* from *sún*, "together with", and *stratiôtēs*, "a soldier". The emphasis here is that Epaphroditus is not only fighting for the faith they both share, but he is fighting with Paul in the particular and specific struggle he faces. In one sense, every follower of Jesus was a fellow-soldier with Paul, but in this moment, Epaphroditus is fighting with him and, by implication, for him. Paul further highlights this when he says of him:

"Welcome him in the Lord with great joy, and honour men like him, because he almost died for the work of Christ, risking his life to make up for the help you could not give me." (Philippians 2:29-30)

As good and strong and gifted as Paul was, he needed people like Timothy, Epaphroditus, Titus, Archippus, Pheobe, Pricilla, Aquila, Andronicus, Junias and Silas, to name but a few. However, we tend to see them as "members of the team" and therefore servants of Paul and the cause. But from the language of Paul to Philippi we see that he regarded Timothy and Epaphroditus (and others like them) as much more than members of the workforce. He saw them as friends.

Like Paul, I could do a "Romans 16" list of people who have stood with me and for me in moments of crisis, pain and brokenness. Friends whose generosity has sustained us, whose courage has inspired us, and whose understanding has comforted us. Solomon was so right when he said, *"Two are better than one..."* and I wish I had the time and the space to talk about each person. But for the purpose of this chapter, and the context of dark valleys specifically referenced within this book, three people are worthy of special mention.

Simon Jarvis – My Brother

"If one falls down, his friend can help him up. But pity the man who falls and has no one to help him up." (Ecclesiastes 4:10)

If I had to pay Simon for the time he has given to me since the summer of 2014 alone, I would need this book to be a bestseller to cover the bill. My own brother passed away in May 2013, and although I had known Simon before then, he has become as a brother to me in every way. If ever there was a *brother born for my adversity* it was him, as over and over again he was there on the phone or in person, to help pick me up. In this season he's faced his own challenges with a growing church, family pressures and some personal health issues which included a minor heart-attack (although he's milked the sympathy on that for all it's worth). On top of all that, he's a West Ham United supporter, which might explain his empathy for those in pain.

As I've journeyed through the dark valley, Simon's contribution to my heart has been significant in three major ways.

Firstly, he believed in me

When things go wrong, or at least not as planned, the on-looking world often uses a maxim that's not actually in the Bible, but it is quoted by some as if it is: "There's no smoke without fire". By this they mean if something is going wrong on the outside, it must be because something bad is happening on the inside. Job's friends particularly liked this idea and on numerous occasions tried to convince Job he had done something to "merit" such disaster in his life, when Job (and God) knew the smoke they saw was not the evidence of a fire!

Simon believed *in me* and he *believed me*. He asked the tough questions and probed me for the truth. But when I told him, he believed me and that was it, settled. When others were questioning what I had done, Simon believed in who I was – and in the worst moments of the journey he kept reminding me of that fact.

"A man of many companions may come to ruin, but there is a friend who sticks closer than a brother." (Proverbs 18:24)

Secondly, challenged me

What I love about Simon is that he's not afraid to get in my face and see how I react, because he's committed to my wellbeing. His challenge has never come in public, in front of others, but always in private, where mercy reigns and his motivation has not been to pull me down, but to lift me up and make me a better man. Over and over, in the journey through the valley, he challenged my attitude, my words, my behaviour and my responses. There were times when he told me I was wrong and other moments when he firmly suggested I could have done something a better way. But on all of those occasions, I didn't feel demeaned or humiliated, rather affirmed and loved. He had earned the right to challenge me, not just because of the miles we had on the clock together, but also because of the spirit with which he spoke. At times his words were bruising, but they always led to blessing.

"Better is open rebuke that hidden love. Wounds from a friend can be trusted, but an enemy multiplies kisses." (Proverbs 27:5-6)

Thirdly, he provoked me

In all our years of friendship I have known one thing about Simon, he wants me to be the best John Andrews I can be. He's never been threatened by my gift, nor I by his, and in it all, he's invested into me so that I can be all I was meant to be. Simon has done an amazing job raising leaders in his local church, across the nation and the world, but that isn't just his job, that's *him*; he passionately loves leaders. I have seen that when the lights are on him, and when no one is looking. I've seen him sow into his leaders in public, and I've benefited from his service in private. Simon didn't just want me to survive (which is better than dying), but he prodded and poked me with love-fuelled provocation, so that I could thrive and succeed.

"As iron sharpens iron, so one man sharpens another." (Proverbs 27:17)

We all need *brothers* (I use the term generically to include women) like this. For no matter how good we think we are, how strong we reckon we might be, we all need to know that someone believes in us (not just our ministry or badge) and will stand with us when the "smoke" is rising. We need *brothers*, even in the valley moments, who will ask the tough questions – not to destroy us, but to help us think and work through what is really going on. We need *brothers* who will provoke us to greatness, sharpening us with their love and passion, so that we can ultimately be the best we can be. Too many in life and ministry stand alone, because we think we can manage, or because we think no one can be that *brother* to us. If Paul needed a *brother*, I think it's a safe bet that we do too.

Dawn Andrews – My Fellow-Worker

"Also, if two lie down together they will keep warm. But how can one keep warm alone?" (Ecclesiastes 4:11)

Outside of deciding to follow Jesus, marrying Dawn Willows was the best decision I ever made. I'd like to say it was the result of great planning, or the outcome of an intentional strategy, but it was really down to the grace-filled "luck of the Lord". I was a third year at Bridal, I mean *Bible* College, and she arrived as a first year... and immediately caught my eye. Within a few weeks she had captured my heart and within a few months I knew she would be my wife (provided she agreed of course). We married in 1988 and what an adventure we've had together. The Lord has been so good to us and our cup has overflowed for sure. But in our recent valleys, Dawn has shone like a beacon of light in the darkness and her attitude and conduct has reminded me again how amazingly blessed I am to have her by my side. She has been my ʿēzĕr – my helper – and although her physical beauty continues to attract me, it is her inner beauty that has truly captivated me. As Solomon so brilliantly concluded,

"Charm is deceptive, and beauty is fleeting; but a woman who fears the Lord is to be praised." (Proverbs 31:30)

As we've journeyed through brokenness, Dawn has helped me find power in the pain as her heart has shone through in the following ways:

Firstly, her servant heart
In the midst of personal pain, when wrestling with a "disappointed" that threatened to become full-blown disappointment, I have seen Dawn, over and over again, get up and serve me and those around her. Her capacity for service is immense, and at times when others should have been serving her, she stepped forward and gave herself. She's a "first in last out" type of person. In every context in which I've seen her serve, she has always given her best and left a situation better than she found it.

There were times in the valley (to my shame) when I tried to get her to pull back, step away and let others do it. But I've learned that such words are hurtful to my "fellow-worker", and that trying to prevent her from serving is like pulling out her tongue! Her servant heart has blessed, inspired and challenged me more times that I can count. Her willingness to serve has empowered me to serve, even when I didn't feel like doing it. In truth, she has served contexts that didn't deserve her and which haven't always treated her as her service deserved – but that has never stopped her from getting up, grabbing the "basin and the towel" and washing the feet of her world.

"She watches over the affairs of her household and does not eat the bread of idleness." (Proverbs 31:27)

Secondly, her generous heart

I caught a glimpse of the generosity I would come to love and appreciate when Dawn was leaving Bible College. In the days before government loans for tuition fees, Dawn had been blessed by a generous gift so she could pay off her fees. But the gift meant she had a substantial amount of money left over – a blessing for us, I thought, as we were about to get married with virtually nothing in the bank. I thought wrong, since Dawn had other ideas. Having been blessed, she found a needy student and promptly gave the whole amount away. Fortunately, this wasn't a one off and her generosity throughout our marriage has been a joy to behold. However, her generosity has continued to shine through in the valleys of recent years. Her eyes are always open to the needs of others, and (mostly in secret) she has opened up her heart, her time, her talents and her purse to those in need. This generous spirit has gone into combat against the poverty mind-set that pain and brokenness has tried to draw us into. Every time I see her open her arms, I'm blessed and inspired and I realise I'm a much better man because I get to live in such a world with such a woman.

"She opens her arms to the poor and extends her hands to the needy." (Proverbs 31:20)

Thirdly, her determined heart

Dawn is a woman of gentle disposition, rarely pushing herself forward and happy to do the "behind the scenes" work, but her gentleness should not be thought of as weakness, for she is one of the most determined people I know. In our journey with Simeon, one moment stands out. We were having a particularly bad weekend with him as the trial loomed closer and his mood swung dramatically back and forth. A relatively minor household issue escalated into a war and, as Simeon and I squared up to one another, Dawn stepped in. Seeing his mother in tears, Simeon ran out the door and Dawn ran after him, telling him repeatedly she loved him and pursuing him down the road.

Perhaps realising he wasn't getting away from her, or because of the overwhelming emotion of the experience, Simeon collapsed in tears at the side of the road and there was Dawn, wrapping her arms around our broken boy, nursing him back to the house. Had Dawn not been there, and not been determined with her love, I dread to think what might have happened. But she was, she did and we're all still together. The strength of her determination has blessed and inspired me. I'm a pretty strong person, but I have had the occasional thought of heading for the hills and leaving the weirdness to someone else. It's her steadfastness that has helped me to stay, stick with it and see it through.

"She is clothed with strength and dignity; she can laugh at the days to come." (Proverbs 31:25)

We all need an ʿēzĕr, a helper who will stand with us no matter what and work with us in the midst of the trials. My reflections have been directed towards my wife, simply because in my world she is my preeminent fellow-worker. However, a fellow-worker need not be a spouse or even a family member, but someone whose heart is for you, and who is determined to stand and work with you. We all need such people in our lives – those with generous, servant hearts that move beyond words and into actions; who demonstrate they are with us by actually standing beside us and staying with us until the job is done.

Paul was a brilliant, highly focused and gifted man, yet he needed a fellow-worker; a side-by-side companion. He found that not in a spouse, but in men such as Epaphroditus. Fellow-workers won't leave us when we enter the valley, they'll stay by our side the whole way through!

Brigitta Goff – My Fellow-Soldier

"Though one may be overpowered, two can defend themselves. A cord of three strands is not quickly broken." (Ecclesiastes 4:12)

The first time I talked with Brigitta I was struck by one thing: she was a fighter. Though she was respectful and listened to my ideas and my point of view, I liked the fact that she wasn't afraid to use her brain or express her opinion. She served well in a specific ministry context I was helping to lead and slowly, over a period of two years or so, we became friends. Little did I know that the woman who gave me a bit of hard time in that first meeting, would become our fellow-soldier through a terrifying valley.

From the very beginning of Simeon's ordeal and eventual trial, Brigitta got involved and her expertise in the law proved invaluable. Although she was never our lawyer, she connected us to good people and helped us to understand what was going on. Just as Epaphroditus fought with, and for, Paul in a specific context of struggle, so Brigitta became a warrior who fought tenaciously for Simeon and our family over every step of the 18-month valley. She became our fellow-soldier and, at times, didn't just fight alongside us, but carried the fight for us, leading the charge when we felt unable to do so. Her fighting spirit came through time and again.

Firstly, her loyalty

When Brigitta picks a cause, she sticks with it until the job is done, and she picked our family and Simeon's case as one of her causes, believing he was innocent from the beginning. Although she was incredibly busy, she always made time for us, even giving us permission to contact her on holiday if we were desperate. Her loyalty was supremely expressed during the week of Simeon's trial, when she took a whole week off work to be with us (as did Claire Spiby, Simeon's friend from college). I will be eternally grateful for that single warrior act, sitting with us through every brutal and terrifying minute of court time; talking us through the bits we did and didn't understand; eating with us and speaking words of life and faith over us. I don't know how much in financial terms that week cost Brigitta, but not once did she complain or make us feel like we were a burden to her. Every day she came, she stayed and she fought alongside us.

"*Love and faithfulness keep a king safe; through love his throne is made secure.*" (Proverbs 20:28)

Secondly her counsel

When we find ourselves lost, there is nothing more comforting than getting directions from someone who knows the way. When it came to Simeon's journey, Brigitta knew the way and her wisdom helped us so much – just being able to talk to someone who knew the law, followed Jesus, was filled with the Spirit and loved my family and me. I remember the night before Simeon took the stand. Brigitta sat with Simeon and myself until after 9pm, going through the details of the case, helping to bring clarity to his thinking. Watching him the next day in the dock, his future in the balance, I saw him benefit from the wise counsel of our warrior friend.

"Make plans by seeking advice; if you wage war, obtain guidance." (Proverbs 20:18)

Thirdly, her confidence

Though she never once shied away from the realities facing us all as we headed to court, she maintained her confidence in the Lord on our behalf, believing that the Lord has a great plan for Simeon's life and that out of this would come the greater glory of His purpose. She spoke to me about my future, reminding me time and again that the trial was a forerunner to the triumph. The morning Simeon was due to take the stand, Brigitta shared a word with us the Lord had given her for him the night before. It would not be prudent to share that word, but its impact was dramatic and enabled us to pray in a focused way for the morning to come. As Simeon took the stand, I saw the spiritual impact of the word Brigitta shared on both him and the wider proceedings of that day. I'm so grateful that Brigitta was obedient to the Lord in not only listening to His word, but helping us put it into practice. Brigitta didn't just fight alongside us with the sword of her own expertise, she fought with spiritual weapons that helped pull down strongholds.

"The wicked man flees though no one pursues, but the righteous are as bold as a lion." (Proverbs 28:1)

We all need some warriors around us as we walk through

the valley; people like Brigitta who will fight for us and alongside us because they believe in us and the justice of our cause. These fellow-soldiers may only come into our lives for one fight, but having them beside us could mean the difference between victory and defeat. I was raised in Belfast and I think I'm spiritually, emotionally and psychologically pretty strong, but I was glad for the soldiers who stood beside me so that I didn't have to face the enemy alone!

As we've seen already, Solomon reminds us:

"A cord of three strands is not quickly broken." (Ecclesiastes 4:12)

The image here is of a rope, the individual strands of which are relatively weak. But when they are intertwined with multiple other strands, it produces something of significant strength. Though I am convinced that it was the Word of God and the Presence of God that filled my heart with strength to walk through the valley, I am also aware that those who walked with me played an invaluable part in saving my heart, my life and my future from the ravages of the fight. I will forever be grateful to the friends I've spoken about in this chapter, and others whose names have remained unmentioned, but none of them will be forgotten. I am thankful for their love, loyalty, wisdom, generosity and prayers – all of which have sustained and strengthened me and ensured that even in the darkest moments of the journey, I never walked alone.

Endnotes
1. Apart from this reference it's used in, Rom.16:3, 9, 21; 1 Cor.3:9; 2 Cor.1:24; 2 Cor.8:23; Phil.4:3; Col.4:11; 1 Thess.3:2, Philemon 1:1, 24 and John uses it in 3 Jn.1:8
2. Also used of Archippus in Philemon 1:2
3. Ecclesiastes 4:9-12

Chapter Eleven
Back Together Again – World

[The Power of Purpose]

"A generous man will prosper;
he who refreshes others will himself be refreshed."
(Proverbs 11:25)

Matthew chapter 14 comes to a climactic conclusion. Jesus is seen to walk on water, His disciples declare Him to be the Son of God, and everyone who touches Him receives their healing. It is natural and normal for our eyes to be drawn to this spectacular crescendo and conveniently forget how the chapter began. If we rewind to the beginning we discover that Herod had put John in prison and, as the result of an overreaching promise, had the man of God beheaded. The story concludes:

"Then they (John's disciples) went and told Jesus." (Matthew 14:12)

How does Jesus react to the brutal execution of a man who was both a relative and the harbinger of His coming?

"When Jesus heard what had happened, He withdrew by boat privately to a solitary place." (v13)

The text does not explicitly say that Jesus was grieving, but it is clearly implied with words like "withdrew", "privately" and "solitary place". Confronted with the death of someone He loved, Jesus showed all the signs of someone grieving their loss. Though His time alone was interrupted by the demands of the crowd, later in the chapter, after ministering to the crowds and sending His disciples on ahead of Him, Jesus returned to the quiet place, perhaps to mourn some more.

"After He dismissed them, He went up on a mountainside by Himself to pray." (Matthew 14:23)

A chapter that finished with glory started with grief – and grief so strong that twice in one passage, Jesus attempted to spend time alone. What moved the agony of human loss to the glory of divine opportunity? How did Jesus go from experiencing the pain of loss to walking on the water as if it was solid ground, and from dealing with His own grief to ministering to the needs of others? The easy, lazy answer is that Jesus was God and therefore just got over it, but the text gives us a significant clue that the answer is more human and accessible.

In between the beginning and end of the chapter, between His grief and the glory we see Jesus giving generously to others in three significant ways. Firstly, He healed the sick (v14), then He fed the hungry (v15-21) and lastly, He comforted the weary (v24-33), all the while coming to terms with the death of John. Glory followed grief because of the power of generosity!

Most of us will have perhaps repeated the maxim, "hurt people, hurt people" – meaning that if we do not address the hurts we have received, there is the danger that our hurts will become the means (deliberately or consequentially) of hurting others. There is truth, of course, in this statement and I have seen people allow their hurt to drive an agenda of pain in their marriages, homes and ministries, to such an extent that it crippled and sometimes destroyed the good around them. However, I want to challenge this well-worn wisdom with what seems like a counter-intuitive idea, rooted in the heart of this text and the rest of Scripture, namely, *giving helps healing.*

It would have been the easiest, most expected thing, for Jesus to have withdrawn completely from people and His purpose, when He heard the news of John, and everyone would have understood the need for time out. Yet, Jesus chose the path of generosity in His moment of pain, when He could have sent the crowd away and ignored the distress of His young disciples. Is it wrong to withdraw and find rest in our grief? Of course not. But as we process our loss, disappointment, pain and brokenness, Jesus shows us through His experience that there is a way to find power in the pain, not only by looking in, but by giving out.

The words of Jesus, *"It is more blessed to give than to receive"* (Acts 20:35), are probably the last words we want to hear when someone has just verbally slapped us, we've lost our job, the news from the doctor isn't good, or the bank balance has more red about it than black. Yet, if this is true, then it must be true on the bad days as well as the good, in times of pain and prosperity, and for the valley floors not just the mountain tops.

Finding the blessing at the heart of generosity in many ways becomes even more crucial in the pain, but it flies in the face of everything we feel and truly want. We want the world to stop, to give to us, and to show some generosity and humanity towards our need. As we've seen in the previous chapter, I believe that will always happen, even if it's in small doses. But if we wait for the world to notice, we might be waiting a long time. If we suspend our giving until "the king's horses and king's men" arrive to put us back together again, then a temporary suspension may become a permanent disposition. Nobody came for Jesus and His world didn't miss a heartbeat as His heart was broken. Instead of waiting to receive, He gave! The essence of His response is captured for us in Matthew 14:14, not only outlining His commitment to His purpose, but the attitude of generosity with which He ministered:

"When Jesus landed and saw a large crowd, He had compassion on them and healed them."

Generosity can move us from grief to glory because...

It Draws Us Away

"When Jesus landed and saw a large crowd..."

The decision to dismiss me from my role as Principal went live on Wednesday 12th October and three days later on the 15th October, a large leaders day was held by my denomination in the area where we lived and ministered. Both my daughters, Elaina and Beth-Anne, were due to serve that day as part of the children's ministry, but it meant, in effect, they would be serving the team who had just sacked their dad. It would have been so easy to tell them what to do, but both Dawn and I gave them the freedom to make their own decision. Without our influence, they both decided they wanted to serve, because they loved the kids and because it was the right thing to do. So on that day, they gave their best to the "crowd", even though they were in pain themselves.

It wasn't important who saw them, acknowledged them, or even encouraged them. What was crucial was that they made a decision for growth in their grief. Their service showed that, sometimes, the best way to heal is not to look in, but to give out. As they served those special children and the denomination that day, for a few glorious moments their eyes were off themselves and onto a greater need and a higher call. Like Jesus, they found power in their pain.

When Jesus got into the boat after hearing the news about John, His heart was understandably heavy and He sought solace in seclusion – perhaps to be alone with a small circle of friends, the presence of God, and His own thoughts. But when He stepped out of the boat He was confronted by a sea of faces and a stark choice: to serve or not to serve? The text makes it clear that Jesus, "… saw a large crowd…" and as He looked at them, He could not look at Himself. Jesus' reaction to what He saw as He stepped out of the boat determined what happened throughout the rest of that day.

Generosity draws us away from ourselves in a healthy, healing way. This is not a denial of our pain, or defiance against our brokenness, but rather a decision to "suspend" our personal needs because we see the need of others. This is Kingdom and kingdom generosity helps healing. I would love to be able to say that I have always been courageous in seeing beyond myself, but I've noticed that when I do give in to me, my healing seems to take a little longer and the process becomes a little harder. Here's what I've observed:

Firstly, when my eyes are on me my vision shrinks
I have discovered that when *I* dominates the horizon my options vastly reduce. Looking inward at my own pain and brokenness feels normal and natural, but if that is the only thing I see, then without knowing it, or feeling it at the time, the vision for my life slowly starts shrinking. I know we won't want to hear this, but we need to see something beyond ourselves if we are to survive and go forward.

I met a young man recently in a church I was ministering in

who, like my son, had struggled with self-harming. He spoke about it in a most disarming way and it was clear from the conversation that he had conquered it. I asked him how he had overcome and he told me that one of the keys was serving others. He found an organisation that helped young people who self-harmed and so he volunteered and gave himself to the "crowd". He told me, "In helping them, I helped myself." His vision could so easily have shrunk to the size of his scars, but instead his horizon expanded as he saw an opportunity to serve.

We must not allow "self" to become the only person in the picture, for to do so will rob us of both opportunity and possibility. When *I* dominates, we can't see the crowd, and without the crowd to draw us out, the only direction we can go is inward, into ourselves. It is more blessed to give than to receive, for when we give, our world grows.

Secondly, when my eyes are on me, my problem(s) magnify

I have discovered that when *I* dominates the horizon, my problems, whatever they are, grow in size and invariably become larger than they are. I don't wish to minimise any challenges you may be going through, but they are tough enough to defeat without making them bigger than they actually are.

This was one of my greatest struggles with the journey towards the trial with Simeon. Such a situation was impossible to ignore, and indeed would have been irresponsible to ignore. But the more I allowed it into my mind, the bigger and more terrifying it became. I remember watching the news and there was a special report on the state of Britain's prisons, which said how our prisons were filled with crime, drugs and disorder. As I watched it, all I could think about was Simeon and the possibility that he might end up in a place like that and I literally felt sick. Had I allowed that to become my focus, I'm not sure I would have made it. But without denying its reality, Dawn and I had to find a "crowd" to focus us; something that wouldn't necessarily take our problem away, but at least challenge its expanding dimensions in our minds.

I have found that generosity doesn't make the problem disappear but it does help put it in its place. Opening our hearts to others and giving whatever we are and have, forces the pain and brokenness back into the box in which it belongs and prevents it from invading the spaces where hope and life live. I know we would rather not have the problem at all, but in the absence of deliverance, we must find a way to keep its terror under control. Generosity is one such way. It is more blessed to give than to receive, for when we give our heart grows.

Thirdly, when my eyes are on me my strength diminishes

I have discovered that when *I* dominates the horizon my ability to resist and fight weakens – mainly because I am looking to myself for solutions that, in instances of pain and brokenness, I just don't have. When people tell me to "pull yourself together" or "get a grip", I have no idea what that means or how it's done. To a person already floundering in the sea of doubt and confusion that pain often brings, those words are like throwing them an anchor in the storm rather than a life-belt.

Solomon tells us that the person who "refreshes others will himself be refreshed" (Proverbs 11:25). A more literal translation might read:

"... *He who waters shall himself be watered.*"

The idea is clear, that if we seek to strengthen, water and refresh others, the Lord will see to it that we ourselves are strengthened, watered and refreshed. This seems like a contradictory idea, for surely if I give out, I will be depleted and the little strength I have will be further diminished? However, the Bible wants us to understand the supernatural power of generosity – that as we give, even out of our weakness, so the Lord will see to it that we are rewarded and renewed in kind.

This is why in the dark valley we have journeyed through, I have refused to quit ministering and giving to others. Because I know that if I give out, if I am generous, if I make it a goal to refresh others, the Lord will see to it that I am supernaturally strengthened and refreshed. From the outside, some may have the opinion that what I do is because I need the work, or have an egotistical craving for acceptance, or that I find my worth in my ministry, but nothing could be further from the truth. I know that if I stop, this will shut down an opportunity through which I can use who I am and what I have to water the "crowd" and, without the crowd ever knowing what I was going through at the time, I will know I gave my best, whatever context I found myself in. Even when my confidence was low, the Lord's water refreshed and strengthened me, as I gave to others.

Pain and brokenness divert our focus naturally onto self, and though there is a time for this, self cannot be the only thing we see. Generosity fights the pull of pain's gravity towards self, and supernaturally endues us with strength to do things we did not think possible. When we cut off the means to give we damage our ability to live. It is more blessed to give than to receive, for when we give our courage grows!

Generosity can move us from grief to glory because,

It Calls Something Out
"… He had compassion on them and healed their sick." (v14)

When Jesus had compassion on the crowd, something deep

and transformative was called out of Him and given by Him. The word Matthew uses for compassion is *splagchnízomai* pointing to feeling something so deeply that it results in action. Every time this word is used of Jesus in the gospels it is always associated with action, because it's not just a feeling, it is connected with what He sees and knows. Jesus wasn't the only one who saw the crowd that day – after all, His disciples were with Him – but He was the only one who had compassion for them. What He felt was not merely because of His personality type or emotional disposition, it was connected to His call and His purpose.

The pain of John's death attempted to muscle its way in and dethrone the purpose for which Jesus was called, so His response of compassion was not just about the needs of the crowd, but about obedience to a greater cause. It is too easy to think of compassion as a feeling that happens to some people and not to others, but of Jesus we read that He "had compassion", not that He felt it. As He stepped out of the boat and looked at the crowd, Jesus' compassion came forth because He made a conscious decision to allow this to be a part of His world and an essential part of His calling. Compassion came out because kingdom generosity was already inside.

Generosity exists at the very core of the value system of the Kingdom of God. In the great sermons Jesus preached on the Mount[1] and the Plain[2] this theology reverberates over and over again:

"So in everything, do to others what you would have them do to you, for this sums up the Law and the Prophets." (Matthew 7:12)

"Give and it will be given to you. A good measure, pressed down, shaken together and running over, will be poured into

your lap. For with the measure you use, it will be measured to you." (Luke 6:38)

These truths weren't given to enable pithy offering talks on a Sunday morning, rather they were designed to form the framework of what the Kingdom is and how it is recognised. At the heart of this Kingdom is generosity and the transformational power it brings. So when we drop back to Matthew 14 and hear how Jesus "had compassion", this should not be a surprise to us. This is the code Jesus lived by, irrespective of feelings or circumstances.

Generosity then, is a decision based on something we know to be true. Circumstances, pain, disappointment and brokenness all attempt to distort this reality, causing us to back away from compassion and generosity in an attempt to convince us that such a road leads to healing. But the Kingdom teaches us that *giving helps healing*, and if we allow it, generosity will call something out of us that pain will tell us is not there.

Look at the generosity of Jesus in the midst of His own grief.

His Generosity Empowered

"… and healed their sick." (v14)

Because Jesus was willing to give, sick people got healed. Their healing was only possible because of the generosity of Jesus that flowed from His compassion. It wasn't just the power of God that healed them; it was the vehicle of His generosity that made it possible.

When writing to the church at Corinth to encourage them in their own generosity, Paul held up the generosity of their Macedonian brothers and sisters as example to them:

"Out of the most severe trial, their overflowing joy and their extreme poverty welled up in rich generosity. For I testify that

they gave as much as they were able, and even beyond their ability." (2 Corinthians 8:2-3)

Just like Jesus, the Macedonians gave generously whilst in their own valley of trial, amidst the brokenness of their own poverty. As a result, many of their brothers and sisters were strengthened. This teaches us that generosity is not only *possible* in the midst of our own dark valley, but it is *necessary* in order to help us escape it. *Giving helps healing.*

His Generosity Enriched

"They all ate and were satisfied..." (v20)

We love the story of Jesus feeding five thousand-plus people that day with baskets full of food left over, but none of this would have happened had Jesus not decided to be generous in His own grief. While the hungry got filled, few of them had any idea of the burden the meal-provider was carrying.

Paul says to Corinth:

"For you know the grace of our Lord Jesus Christ, that though He was rich, yet for your sakes He became poor, so that you through His poverty might become rich." (2 Corinthians 8:9)

Enriching others challenges the reality of our own impoverishment, whether that be material, emotional or psychological. Even though we are *poor*, because of the valley we are in, a commitment to generosity helps break the attitude of poverty that so often stalks in the shadows of difficulty. To be poor and to have an attitude of poverty are two different things and only go hand in hand when we let them. It is possible, like the Macedonians and like Jesus, to be in a place of poverty and pain, but not be impoverished by them! That's why helping to satisfy the needs of others when we have needs of our own is one of the great keys of maintaining a good heart on the valley floor. *Giving helps healing.*

His Generosity Enlarged

"Then Peter got down out of the boat, walked on the water and came towards Jesus." (v29)

Peter only got out of the boat because of Jesus' invitation and that only happened because Jesus was walking on the water, and that only happened because when Jesus was alone in prayer and mourning Mark tells us,

"He saw the disciples straining at the oars, because the wind was against them." (Mark 6:48)

There's that idea again: *He saw.* When most of us would have had our eyes closed in prayer or the sleep of grief, Jesus' eyes were opened to the needs of His friends and He went to them on the water. That in turn enabled Peter to walk on water (if only for a little while) and experience the supernatural power of God's word. When Peter got back into the boat, he would never be the same again, for he had done something that, as a seasoned fisherman, he knew was impossible. We focus on Peter walking on the water, but remember, the One who called him onto the water and eventually saved him from it, had just been grieving the loss of John. One of the most spectacular miracles in the gospels happened off the back of bad news and occurred in the crucible of grief. *Giving helps healing.*

His Generosity Encouraged

"Truly You are the Son of God." (v33)

With Peter back in the boat and the raging storm now calmed, the young disciples saw Jesus in a very different light. In Matthew's Gospel this is the first time they express any confession of their belief in Jesus as the Son of God, and they do so because of what they've just experienced. Their view of Him changed because of what He did for them. Jesus was able to calm their storm because in some measure He had calmed His own, soothing the call of grief long enough to sooth the fears of His friends and give them courage. They thought they were alone and maybe even lost, but His presence with them changed everything as His generosity calmed the storm of their hearts. *Giving helps healing.*

Helping others be their best when we are not feeling the best about ourselves is part of the call and challenge of generosity. It's back to the realisation that our weakness can be a vehicle for God's strength and that through our vulnerability He can perform great things.

Part of my role when I worked at the Bible College was to lead one of the annual missions trips. In April 2016 I took a team to Aberdeen where we served King's Church and Teen Challenge. It was a great trip and everything the team got involved in was a blessing, with outstanding ministry at many levels happening over the ten days we were there.

However, right in the middle of that trip (in fact as I was having a coffee with the Senior Pastor), I received a call from Brigitta to tell me that Simeon was in a terrible state and I needed to speak to him urgently. That day he and Dawn were due to meet the barrister who was going to help us with our case, and as far as we were concerned, it was a simple, routine meeting. However, fear and panic had gripped my son and he was now considering taking a plea – something that shocked us all. As he came onto the phone, he was crying and I tried not to join him.

"Why do you want to take the plea son?" I asked.

"Because this is destroying everyone and I just want to get it over with."

I calmed him down and then said,

"Okay, I'm going to ask you one question. If this is the only time in your life you tell me the truth, then please be totally honest with me." He agreed.

"Did you do it or not?" I asked.

His answer was immediate and emphatic:

"No Dad, I didn't!"

"Then don't take the plea. We'll get through this."

Though another seven months of pain was to come, we are all so glad he didn't take the plea.

As I sat down to finish my coffee with the pastor he had no idea what had just happened. Not a single member of my team knew what I or my family were going through at that stage. Yet, that missions trip remains one of the happiest, most blessed and fulfilling trips I've ever had … and I've had a few. As I served the team and sat with drug addicts in recovery, as we painted school toilets and the reception hall of the local YMCA, as we ministered in the church through preaching, teaching and hosting I was reminded again:

"It is more blessed to give than to receive."

I understood afresh that giving helps healing and that an act of generosity doesn't just empower, enrich, enlarge or encourage those to whom we give, but the benefits to the giver are immeasurable. So often we think of the rewards of giving in material or physical terms, but I believe, as we've seen, there can be a return to the giver that helps grow our world, our hearts and our courage.

Matthew chapter 14 began with grief, but ended with glory – all because of the power of generosity demonstrated in the valley of brokenness and the crucible of pain. I pray that wherever you are, you will find the power to give; that in the act of pouring water on others, you also will be watered. May you discover that *giving helps healing.*

Endnotes
1. Matthew chapters 5-7
2. Luke chapter 6

Chapter Twelve
Changing the Past

"You intended to harm me, but God intended it for good..."
(Genesis 50:20)

Looking back is only possible once we've gone through. There are some lessons that we learn and understand while we walk in the valley. But there are other truths and conclusions of faith that can only be reached once we are beyond the trial of pain and looking back. So often we look for meaning and explanation whilst in the midst of our brokenness, but greater clarity has come to me as I've moved beyond a particular experience to see it from a different perspective.

When Joseph finally confronted the brothers who had abused him and abandoned him to slavery twenty-two years previously, he did so as a man not trapped in the pain of brokenness, but rather as one who had journeyed beyond his darkest valley to a place of rest and freedom. Read his words carefully:

"I am your brother Joseph, the one you sold into Egypt! And now, do not be distressed and do not be angry with yourselves for selling me here, because it was to save lives that God sent me ahead of you. For two years now there has been famine in

the land, and for the next five years there will not be ploughing or reaping. But God sent me ahead of you to preserve for you a remnant on earth and to save your lives by a great delivery. So then, it was not you who sent me here, but God. He made me father to Pharaoh, lord of his entire household and ruler of all Egypt." (Genesis 45:4-8)

In Joseph's narrative the story has subtly but powerfully changed. Twice he reminds his brothers of what they did:

"... the one *you sold* into Egypt!"

"... for *selling me* here..."

However, over the scars those irrefutable facts left, Joseph had imprinted a new life, transforming their meaning:

"... God *sent* me ahead of you..."

"But God *sent* me ahead of you..."

"... it was not you who *sent* me here, but God..."

In Joseph's reinterpretation of the past, the fact that he was *sold* (referenced twice) is eclipsed by the belief that he was *sent* (referenced three times). Though the facts remained the same, Joseph changed the meaning and, in doing so, changed everything.

The Psalmist also highlights this very same tension in the story when he says:

"...and He (the Lord) *sent* a man before them – Joseph, *sold* as a slave." (Psalm 105:17)

Note the juxtaposition in the two accounts. In Genesis, *sold* comes before *sent*, because in Joseph's experience, that's how it happened. He was stripped, beaten, humiliated and *sold*, with his feet "bruised with shackles" and his neck "put in irons".[1] Then later, much later, he understood that the Lord had actually *sent* him for a greater purpose. However, it is Joseph's interpretation of the past that then influences the Psalmist, who places *sent* before *sold*. Future generations would understand Joseph as a *sent one*, not because of *their* interpretation of the story, but because of *his*.

But if the past is the past, can it really be changed? In one sense, of course, it cannot, as the facts of our lives remain forever set in stone. Our yesterdays will always be part of us and there is no denying that reality. However, we can change the meaning of the past. Or, put another way, how we see it, understand it and then respond and relate to it.

Addressing the experiences of our past is crucial as we negotiate today and plan for the future, because wherever we go and whatever we do our past will go with us. But the power our past is allowed to wield is determined not by what happened *to us then*, but by what is happening *in us now*. Yesterday's influence over today is, in some ways, determined by my interpretation of yesterday. Thus, how I see what has been becomes a part of my journey of faith. When Joseph looked back he saw *sent* over *sold* and though the facts remained the same, the meaning changed. If we can change the meaning of what has been, we can change the past!

But how did Joseph change his past?

From the text it seems he did two main things. Though they are neither simple nor easy, I believe they are keys to finding new meaning in the past and fresh hope for our future.

Forgiveness – He Let Go

Unforgiveness will fog our view of the past. Therefore we have to find a way to address those who hurt us, disappointed us, abandoned us or betrayed us. This is the first and vital step to being able to look back and find new meaning. If we are not prepared to release those who have wounded us, then we will be forever chained to the facts as they happened. Had Joseph not forgiven his brothers, then his narrative would have been stuck on the word *sold;* stuck on the facts of what they did.

We're not sure when Joseph came to a place of forgiveness, but there are two insights that show it may have taken a while before he truly settled the issue. The first occurred while he was in prison where he interpreted the dreams of the baker and the cupbearer. In making his appeal to the latter he says,

"... remember me... For I was forcibly carried off from the land of the Hebrews, and even here I have done nothing to deserve being put in a dungeon." (Genesis 40:14-15)

Although he is kind to his brothers in that he does not implicate them at this stage, a sense of injustice still rides strong in the young man. Even though the text says that the Lord was with him in both Potiphar's house and the prison, there is no indication in Joseph's language at this stage that he "feels" sent by God to do anything.

The second occurs when Joseph is in the service of Pharaoh. He takes a wife and in the seven years of plenty they have two sons together. The first son is named, Manasseh, called such according to Joseph:

"... because God has made me forget all my trouble and all my father's household." (Genesis 41:51)

Attempting to forget what happened and who did it to us is not forgiveness, because forgiveness does not eradicate the facts, it faces them. Joseph understandably wanted to forget the pain and the betrayal, but in forgetting his father's household he was in danger of forgetting the God-given dreams that set these events in motion in the first place. It is fascinating that when he meets some of his brothers for the first time the text says,

"Then he remembered his dreams about them..." (Genesis 42:9)

Yet it is clear, by the time we get to chapter 45, if there was any doubt that Joseph had forgiven them, it is dispelled in the words we've read earlier in this chapter. Joseph had to move from forgetting to truly forgiving.

Letting go of the past is not about forgetting what has happened, but about facing the facts and forgiving what has happened. There is no doubt that true forgiveness helps us forget, because it allows us to move certain memories to the "back of our minds", so their remembrance no longer has power over us. But we must not confuse an attempt to forget that something happened, or forget a painful season in our lives, as the same thing as forgiveness, for they are not.

Forgiving others is possible if we want to do it, but it's certainly not easy and, in my experience, it has always demanded two attitudes from me.

Honesty

Pretending it doesn't hurt when it does seems like the brave thing to do, but when it comes to forgiving others and changing our past, it is totally unhelpful. I see this a lot in the Church where good people try to draw attention away from themselves by suggesting they are okay, or that things aren't that bad. Of course, there is a time and a place to be honest with how we feel, but let's stop pretending that there's no pain when there is.

In my journey, I have found the value of creating a place of mercy into which I can invite friends I trust. We must only bare our souls in the most sacred of places where mercy reigns and whatever needs to be said can be said. The place of mercy is safe and secure. It's where I am able to say exactly how I feel without being judged and where nothing I say will be repeated without the mutual consent of all involved. Only a few trusted friends or professionals should be invited into this place, but those who are present must be given the freedom to listen, respond and challenge us towards forgiveness and healing. The place of mercy is a place of nakedness where no lies are told and no pretence encouraged.

Do you have such a place? Do you have access to friends or counsellors who can sit with you in your nakedness and hear your confession? It is not impossible to be honest without such a place and people, but it becomes much more difficult. In my darkest valley, the place of mercy has saved my soul as friends I trust have walked with me.

Humility

When injustice kicks in, so usually does pride. In the English word "pride" notice that "I" is at the centre. This represents one of our greatest challenges when coming to a place of forgiveness. When pride reigns, the agenda of self dominates and this has a tendency to colour our reactions and decisions. If *I* is at the centre of any journey, it is always going to be harder to let go and forgive others.

Over the last few years, as I've walked through some of the greatest challenges of my life, the temptation has been to fight. But if I'm honest, most of the desire to fight has been about my own ego and the defence of my reputation, rather than the honour of the Lord's name or the glory of His cause. It's so easy to get our ego and our cause confused, especially when our call to minister is at the heart of our purpose and inextricably linked to the person we are. There are, of course, times to fight, but before we climb into battle we must always ask ourselves honestly, *what we are fighting for?*

Joseph didn't fight, he served, and he did so with such

humility that in each context in which he served, he not only experienced the favour of the Lord, but promotion from men. Had Joseph been consumed with fighting over his past, I suspect his future would have been lost.

Is it time to let *I* go, to stop fighting for yourself and to start leaning on the Lord who has your best interests in the palm of His hand? Is it time to forgive and release yourself from what they did to you? Injustice, pain, disappointment and hurt will bang on the door of our hearts, hoping that pride will come out to play, but humility will keep the door locked ensuring ego is grounded.

Faith – He Took Hold

One of the greatest acts of faith in anyone's life is when they are prepared to accept a different version of their dreams than the one they had originally hoped for. When we set out with God's promise in our hearts, all of us fell into the temptation of imagining how it was going to work out. I'm pretty certain none of our versions involved cancer, sickness, unemployment, poverty, self-harming, drugs, divorce, death or visits to Crown Court. Yet, so many good and kind followers of Jesus find their journey hijacked by unexpected and unpleasant things which look nothing like their original plan.

Joseph had two dreams that made life look incredible for him. The "interpretation" suggested that he would rise while those around him did a lot of bowing.[2] As a seventeen year old with the status of being his father's favourite, he must have imagined how and when those dreams would play out. Without knowing what his thoughts were, I'm pretty certain they didn't involve slavery, false imprisonment and abandonment. Yet that became his reality and a challenge to his faith to maintain a grip on the dreams and the promises of God, while negotiating a path that must have been beyond his darkest nightmare. Somehow, by faith, Joseph came to understand two profound truths, which helped him change his past.

God's power was greater than theirs

There is a striking contrast between the Joseph of Genesis 37 and the Joseph of Genesis 45. When we meet the seventeen-year-old Joseph with his coat and his dreams, God's name is not mentioned once in the whole of the chapter. Even though we know the Lord gave Joseph the dreams, at no point does he make any acknowledgement to God for these promises. Yet, when we meet the thirty-nine-year-old Joseph, surrounded by the magnificent pomp of Egypt, in a few short moments with his brothers he mentions God five times directly, and it could be argued that His presence dominates the unspoken sub-text.

At the beginning Joseph's faith saw only dreams, but now as a ruler in Egypt his faith saw God at work: "... you sold... but God sent..." Throughout his story it looked like Joseph was at the mercy of people's whims and decisions, a victim of the agenda of others, but by faith he realised this was not the case. The Lord was at work all along, demonstrating that His power was greater than that of his brothers, the captain's or the Pharaoh's.

Only faith can see the reality of God's power at work when it seems as though people have had their way and won the day. With our natural eyes we are consumed with the cruelty of *brothers*, the deceit of *Potiphar's wife* and the apathy of the *cupbearer*. But by faith we can see the hand of the Lord at work in each and every moment to bring his purpose to bear. I love how Peter Scazzero puts it:

"In retrospect, I can see in my own life what I could not see at the time; how the job I lost helped me find work I needed to do; and the 'road closed' signed turned me toward terrain I needed to travel: how losses that felt irredeemable forced me to discern meanings I needed to know. On the surface it seemed that life was lessening, but silently and lavishly the seeds of new life were always being sown."[3]

The Lord's power is greater than any scheme that is operating around us right now. Remember, people may make decisions, but it is the Lord who makes destinies. Our lives are not in the hands of people, with their short-term schemes and selfish agendas, but in the hands of the Lord who sees the end from the beginning and is never taken by surprise by anything people may do. He's got you and the work He started in you; He will finish ... His way!

God's plan was bigger than him

When we read the words of Joseph to his brothers and family in Genesis 37 and contrast them with his opening discourse in Genesis 45, we notice another striking change. As a seventeen-year-old the spoken and unspoken narrative is all about him, namely his dreams and how his world will bow to him (even his dad struggled with that one). Whereas the thirty-nine-year-old Joseph speaks about his position and influence for the benefit of his brothers and family:

"... it was to save lives God sent me ahead of you." (Genesis 45:5)

"... to preserve for you a remnant on earth and to save your lives..." (v7)

"You shall live in the region on Goshen..." (v10)

"I will provide for you there..." (v11)

By faith, Joseph looked back and saw why the Lord gave him the dreams and sent him ahead to Egypt. By faith he realised that God's plan was not just about him, but about a much bigger world that the Lord would use him to save. Somewhere in Potiphar's house, the prison or the palace, faith released Joseph from the burden that God's plan was all about him and let him see his life beyond the bounds of success or failure and victory or defeat.

Only faith can help us to see that the plan that has our name on it isn't only about us! Too often we reduce God's purposes down to the life of an individual. We make it about the happiness and success of one person, but His plans are always much bigger. In helping us see the big picture of God's purpose, faith empowers us to address our short-term pain within this context, and thus lifts our vision beyond the now into something greater.

If it is true that the plan God has for us is bigger than us, then it is within His interests to get us where He needs us to be in order to facilitate something that is much greater than us all. Rather than diminish our importance or value, the knowledge that we are part of something bigger should encourage and inspire us. Our dark valley is not a sign that the Lord has forgotten us or made a mistake with us, or that somehow our individual plan is off course. Rather, He will not allow the dark valley to destroy the part in the plan that He wants us to play.

On the 12th May 2017 I sat in a tattoo parlour as my son Simeon had a very special tattoo inked onto his body. Though the image looks amazing (the half face of a lion) it's the positioning and reason for the tattoo that makes it truly special. Simeon had it placed over his left forearm, the area most scared by the effects of his self-harming, to declare that he would never self-harm again. The tattoo was not an attempt to cover over the scars, for they are still visible to sight and touch, but rather to give them new meaning and perhaps a more redemptive purpose. The lion on his forearm hasn't changed the facts of his self-harming, nor the memory of a dark and desperate season in all our lives, but it has given new meaning to the pain and it creates the opportunity for blessing to come from the brokenness. As his father, I struggled to look at his scarred forearm, a reminder of my failure and the depth of his pain. But now, I look at his arm all the time, drawn to the face of the lion and the redemption it offers.

Looking back through the eyes of faith and giving meaning to what has been is no less powerful than being able to look forward and believe for what will be. We think that looking back requires no faith at all, just the ability to remember, but as we've seen, faith can bring purpose and life to facts that once held only disappointment and death. As Joseph concluded at the end of his life:

"You intended it to harm me, but God intended it for good, to accomplish what is now being done, the saving of many lives." (Genesis 50:20)

It is possible to change the past and to look back and see it redemptively, unfettered by the pain of loss and the sorrow of brokenness. But this will only be possible if, like Joseph, we are prepared to let go through forgiveness and take hold by faith. The enemy of our souls wants us to die, or live so crippled by disappointment that the life the Lord designed us to live is lost somewhere in the darkness of the valley floor. Don't give in to the pain and don't give up the cause for which you have been called, for the Lord is for you. He is with you and He will never leave you.

My prayer is that the message of this book has been an encouragement to you; a reminder that you are not Humpty Dumpty and that you *can* be put back together. Like the little bird on my patio, I believe you can and will fly again. That you can find power in the pain and move beyond the brokenness that grips you. There aren't always answers in the valley, and it's okay to admit that sometimes #noneofthismakessense, but I have discovered that in it all, the Lord will never let us go and that His love endures forever.

"Though I walk in the midst of trouble, You preserve my life;
You stretch out Your hand against the anger of my foes,
with Your right hand You save me.
The Lord will fulfil His purpose for me;
Your love, O Lord, endures forever –
do not abandon the works of Your hands."
(Psalm 138:7-8)

Endnotes
1. Psalm 105:18
2. See Genesis 37 for the dreams in full
3. David Shearman quotes Peter Scazzero in his book, *A Verse to Live By*, River Publishing & Media Ltd, 2016, p.74

Simeon's lion face tattoo

About the Author

John has been in full-time Church leadership since 1987. Though called to the UK, John has ministered in over 30 nations of the world with a passion to equip and inspire leaders as well as empower followers of Jesus into effective lifestyle and service.

After leaving Bible School, he helped pioneer and repurpose a church in the village of Havercroft, West Yorkshire, serving there from 1987-1997. From Havercroft he moved to Rotherham New Life in South Yorkshire, (now called the Hub Christian Community), where he helped repurpose that church into a vibrant missional community, serving from 1997-2012. In 2012 John joined the team of Renewal Christian Centre in Solihull, where he served as the Senior Associate Leader until the end of 2014. John also served as the Principal of the British Assemblies of God Bible College, leaving at the end of 2016. He is now part of One Church where he serves the team (www.thisisonechurch.com) whilst also travelling extensively, engaging his passion to teach the Word of God, inspiring a generation of Jesus followers to love Him and serve their world.

Born in Belfast, Northern Ireland, John is married Dawn and together they have three children, Elaina (married to Dan), Simeon and Beth-Anne, not forgetting Pepperoni and Salami (the sausage dogs). John has authored 13 books to date (see **www.drjohnandrews.co.uk** for further details) and his hobbies include supporting his beloved football team, Liverpool, listening to music, reading and watching great movies. He loves to eat and among his favourite food groups are, Chinese, Thai and chocolate!

Printed in Great Britain
by Amazon